W9-AAT-805

Major Muslim Nations

LIBYA

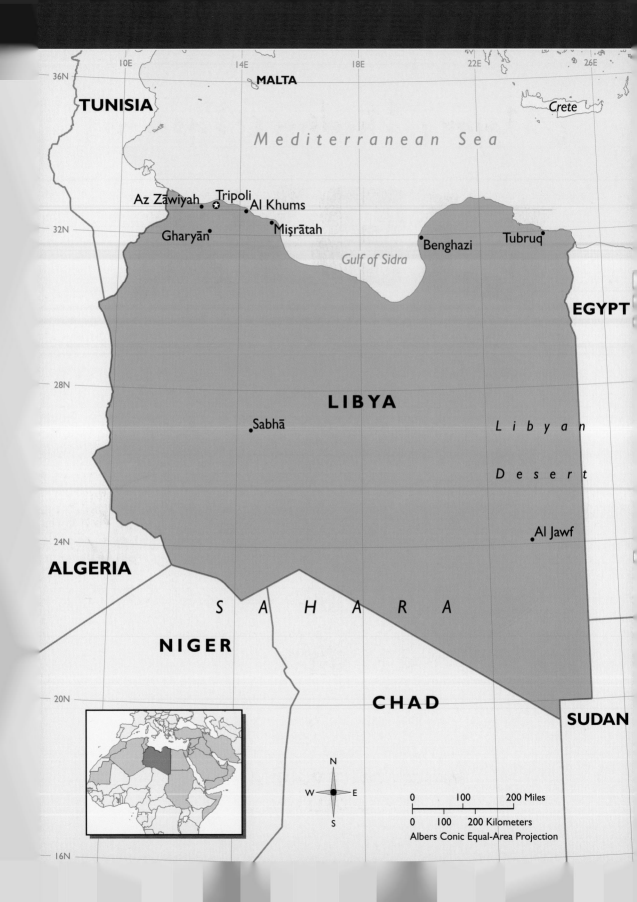

Major Muslim Nations

LIBYA

يجي تـرفض
الابـتزاز

DANIEL E. HARMON

MASON CREST PUBLISHERS
PHILADELPHIA

Mason Crest Publishers
370 Reed Road
Broomall, PA 19008
www.masoncrest.com

Copyright © 2010 by Mason Crest Publishers. All rights reserved.
Printed and bound in the Hashemite Kingdom of Jordan.

First printing

1 3 5 7 9 8 6 4 2

Library of Congress Cataloging-in-Publication Data

Harmon, Daniel E.
  Libya / Daniel E. Harmon.
      p. cm. — (Major Muslim Nations)
    ISBN 978-1-4222-1388-9 (hardcover) — ISBN 978-1-4222-1418-
3 (pbk.)
   1. Libya—Juvenile literature. I. Title.
   DT215.H34 2008
   961.2—dc22
                                                  2008041226

Original ISBN: 1-59084-512-9 (hc)

Major Muslim Nations

TABLE OF CONTENTS

Introduction 7
  Harvey Sicherman, The Foreign Policy Research Institute

Place in the World.................................13

The Land 19

History...29

Politics, the Economy, and Religion 51

The People...71

Communities 85

Foreign Relations 95

Chronology...108

Glossary 110

Further Reading...112

Internet Resources 113

Index 114

Major Muslim Nations

AFGHANISTAN

ALGERIA

BAHRAIN

EGYPT

INDONESIA

IRAN

IRAQ

ISLAM IN ASIA:
   FACTS AND FIGURES

ISLAMISM AND TERRORIST
   GROUPS IN ASIA

ISRAEL

JORDAN

THE KURDS

KUWAIT

LEBANON

LIBYA

MALAYSIA

MIDDLE EAST:
   FACTS AND FIGURES

MOROCCO

PAKISTAN

PALESTINIANS

QATAR

SAUDI ARABIA

SOMALIA

SUDAN

SYRIA

TUNISIA

TURKEY

UAE

YEMEN

Dr. Harvey Sicherman, president and director of the Foreign Policy Research Institute, is the author of such books as *America the Vulnerable: Our Military Problems and How to Fix Them* (2002) and *Palestinian Autonomy, Self-Government and Peace* (1993).

Introduction

by Dr. Harvey Sicherman

America's triumph in the Cold War promised a new burst of peace and prosperity. Indeed, the decade between the demise of the Soviet Union and the destruction of September 11, 2001, seems in retrospect deceptively attractive. Today, of course, we are more fully aware—to our sorrow—of the dangers and troubles no longer just below the surface.

The Muslim identities of most of the terrorists at war with the United States have also provoked great interest in Islam and the role of religion in politics. A truly global religion, Islam's tenets are held by hundreds of millions of people from every ethnic group, scattered across the globe. It is crucial for Americans not to assume that Osama bin Laden's ideas are identical to those of most Muslims, or, for that matter, that most Muslims are Arabs. Also, it is important for Americans to understand the "hot spots" in the Muslim world because many will make an impact on the United States.

A glance at the map establishes the extraordinary coverage of our authors. Every climate and terrain may be found and every form of human society, from the nomads of the Central Asian steppes and Arabian deserts to highly sophisticated cities such as Cairo and Singapore. Economies range from barter systems to stock exchanges, from oil-rich countries to the thriving semi-market powers, such as India, now on the march. Others have built wealth on service and shipping.

The Middle East and Central Asia are heavily armed and turbulent. Pakistan is a nuclear power, Iran threatens to become one, and Israel is assumed to possess a small arsenal. But in other places, such as Afghanistan and the Sudan, the horse and mule remain potent instruments of war. All have a rich history of conflict, domestic and international, old and new.

Governments include dictatorships, democracies, and hybrids without a name; centralized and decentralized administrations; and older patterns of tribal and clan associations. The region is a veritable encyclopedia of political expression.

Although such variety defies easy generalities, it is still possible to make several observations.

First, the regional geopolitics reflect the impact of empires and the struggles of post-imperial independence. While centuries-old history is often invoked, the truth is that the modern Middle East political system dates only from the 1920s, when the Ottoman Empire dissolved in the wake of its defeat by Britain and France in World War I. States such as Algeria, Iraq, Israel, Jordan, Kuwait, Saudi Arabia, Syria, Turkey, and the United Arab Emirates did not exist before 1914—they became independent between 1920 and 1971. Others, such as Egypt and Iran, were dominated by foreign powers until well after World War II. Few of the leaders of these states were happy with the territories they were assigned or the borders, which were often drawn by Europeans. Yet the system has endured despite many efforts to change it.

A similar story may be told in South Asia. The British Raj dissolved into India and Pakistan in 1947. Still further east, Malaysia shares a British experience but Indonesia, a Dutch invention, has its own European heritage. These imperial histories weigh heavily upon the politics of the region.

The second observation concerns economics, demography, and natural resources. These countries offer dramatic geographical contrasts: vast parched deserts and high mountains, some with year-round snow; stone-hard volcanic rifts and lush semi-tropical valleys; extremely dry and extremely wet conditions, sometimes separated by only a few miles; large permanent rivers and wadis, riverbeds dry as a bone until winter rains send torrents of flood from the mountains to the sea.

Although famous historically for its exports of grains, fabrics, and spices, most recently the Muslim regions are known more for a single commodity: oil. Petroleum is unevenly distributed; while it is largely concentrated in the Persian Gulf and Arabian Peninsula, large oil fields can be found in Algeria, Libya, and further east in Indonesia. Natural gas is also abundant in the Gulf, and there are new, potentially lucrative offshore gas fields in the Eastern Mediterranean.

This uneven distribution of wealth has been compounded by demographics. Birth rates are very high, but the countries with the most oil are often lightly populated. Over the last decade, a youth "bulge" has emerged and this, combined with increased urbanization, has strained water supplies, air quality, public sanitation, and health services throughout the Muslim world. How will these young people be educated? Where will they work? A large outward migration, especially to Europe, indicates the lack of opportunity at home.

In the face of these challenges, the traditional state-dominated economic strategies have given way partly to experiments with "privatization" and foreign investment. But economic progress has come slowly, if at all, and most people have yet to benefit from "globalization," although there are pockets of prosperity, high technology (notably in Israel), and valuable natural resources (oil, gas, and minerals). Rising expectations have yet to be met.

A third important observation is the role of religion in the Middle East. Americans, who take separation of church and state for granted, should know that most countries in the region either proclaim their countries to be Muslim or allow a very large role for that religion in public life. (Islamic law, Sharia, permits people to practice Judaism and Christianity in Muslim states but only as *dhimmi*, "protected" but second-class citizens.) Among those with predominantly Muslim populations, Turkey alone describes itself as secular and prohibits avowedly religious parties in the political system. Lebanon was a Christian-dominated state, and Israel continues to be a Jewish state. Even where politics are secular, religion plays an enormous role in culture, daily life, and legislation.

Islam has deeply affected every state and people in these regions. But Islamic practices and groups vary from the well-known Sunni and Shiite groups to energetic Salafi (Wahhabi) and Sufi movements. Over the last 20 years especially, South and Central Asia have become battlegrounds for competing Shiite (Iranian) and Wahhabi (Saudi) doctrines, well financed from abroad and aggressively antagonistic toward non-Muslims and each other. Resistance to the Soviet war in Afghanistan brought these groups battle-tested warriors and organizers responsive to the doctrines made popular by Osama bin Laden and others. This newly significant struggle within Islam, superimposed on an older Muslim history, will shape political and economic destinies throughout the region and beyond.

We hope that these books will enlighten both teacher and student about the critical "hot spots" of the Muslim world. These countries would be important in their own right to Americans; arguably, after 9/11, they became vital to our national security. And the enduring impact of Islam is a crucial factor we must understand. We at the Foreign Policy Research Institute hope these books will illuminate both the facts and the prospects.

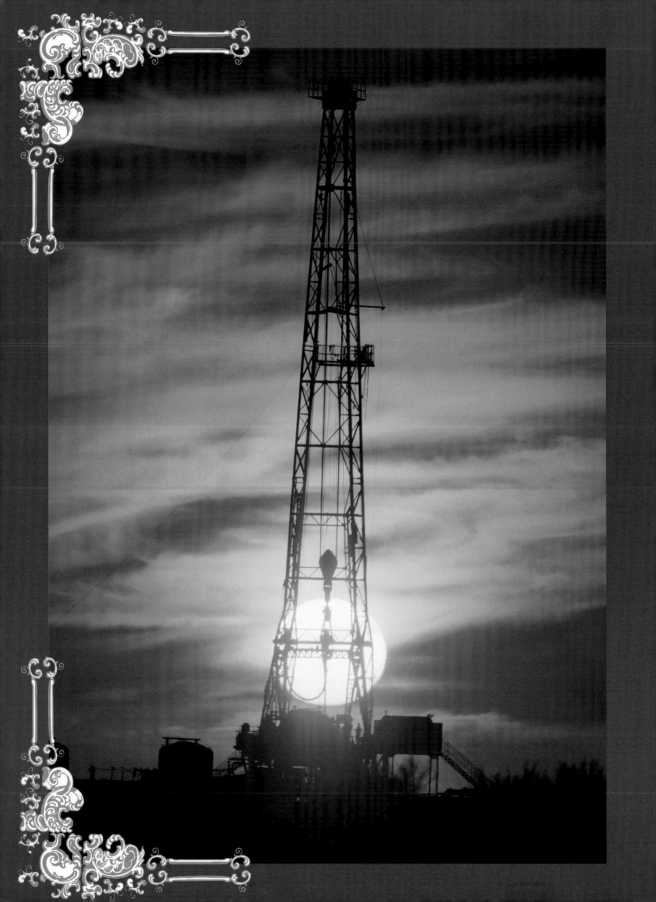

The sun sets over an oil drilling rig in Libya. The North African country sits on a huge amount of oil. After the United Nations and the United States lifted sanctions on Libya in 2003 and 2004, respectively, major oil companies stepped up exploration efforts for oil and natural gas in the country.

Place in the World

Libya, located to the west of Egypt in the middle of North Africa's Sahara Desert, is an uncommonly harsh land. In a country whose area exceeds that of Alaska, there is virtually no surface water.

But Libya does have—in abundance—another liquid under its desert sands: oil. And that oil is of the high-quality, low-sulfur variety—what the petroleum industry refers to as "sweet" crude. With proven reserves of more than 29 billion barrels—an estimated 2 percent of all the untapped petroleum in the world—Libya could be a highly prosperous nation with a significant voice in Arab, African, and world affairs. It isn't. And that has everything to do with the nation's fiery and unpredictable—some observers would say bizarre—leader of more than three decades: Colonel Muammar al-Qaddafi. (His name is rendered many other ways in English, among the more common being Moammar Qadhafi and Mu'ammar Gadhafi.)

THE GREAT SOCIALIST PEOPLE'S LIBYAN ARAB JAMAHIRIYA

Not until the middle of the 20th century did "Libya" come to refer to the Arab nation that borders the Mediterranean Sea on the north, Egypt on the east, Sudan on the southeast, Chad and Niger on the south, Algeria on the west, and Tunisia on the northwest. But the term has been in use since ancient times: the Egyptians knew a particular Berber tribe to the west of their lands as "Libyans." When the Greeks arrived to colonize the region, they referred to all of northern Africa to the west of Egypt as "Libye." And during the latter part of the Roman occupation that followed, around A.D. 300, Emperor Diocletian designated the Cyrenaica region (what is today northeastern Libya) as two separate provinces: Libya Superior ("Upper Libya") and Libya Inferior ("Lower Libya").

But "Libya" is only the short form of the modern North African nation's name. The official name is the Great Socialist People's Libyan Arab Jamahiriya—a name that was bestowed by Muammar Qaddafi and that, in some respects, reflects the contradictions of his rule.

"Socialist" refers to an economic and political system, called *socialism*, in which the government or the people collectively (rather than individuals) own the country's businesses and industries and control the production and distribution of goods (in theory for the benefit of the people). This idea runs contrary to the economic system that prevails in the United States, which is referred to as "capitalism" or "free enterprise." Under this system, individuals own property and run businesses for profit, and market forces, not the government, determine which goods are produced and how they are distributed.

As an economic theory socialism resembles—and, in the minds

of some people, is almost indistinguishable from—**communism**, which likewise opposes free enterprise and private property. As a political system communism is associated especially with the People's Republic of China and the former Soviet Union—repressive, undemocratic, **totalitarian** regimes.

Qaddafi has publicly rejected communism—though, with characteristic inconsistency, he has borrowed heavily from its symbols and themes. In the early 1970s, for example, he proclaimed a "cultural revolution" to transform Libyan society—echoing the 1960s Cultural Revolution of Communist China's Mao Zedong. Mao's collected wisdom is found in the Little Red Book; to explain his worldview Qaddafi penned *The Green Book* (green being the traditional color of the Islamic religion). Red Square dominates Moscow, the capital of the former Soviet Union (and now Russia); Qaddafi made Green Square the focus of Tripoli, the Libyan capital. More significantly, Qaddafi maintains the fiction that there is no government in Libya, a situation that mirrors the supposed final stage of communism—the "withering away of the state."

Libyan leader Muammar al-Qaddafi, wearing gold robes and a skull cap, leaves an Arab League summit in Amman, Jordan. Qaddafi has ruled in Libya since leading a September 1969 uprising that forced King Idris al-Sanusi from the throne. Qaddafi is a complex leader—he has been condemned in the West for his support of terrorism, but praised by some in the Middle East for his efforts to unify the Arab world.

But if Qaddafi officially rejected communism (despite many contradictions), he also rejected U.S. and Western-style capitalism and representative government. Western political systems, he maintained, "falsify genuine democracy" by, for example, giving power to political figures who have received only a portion of the public's vote—possibly as little as 51 percent. This, he declared, is really dictatorship.

True democracy, he stated, is achieved only when the people rule themselves—as in the Libyan *jamahiriya*, a term Qaddafi himself coined and that is translated as "government through the masses" or "state of the masses." Thus Qaddafi officially holds no government title or position.

Once again, however, the contradictions abound. The man who has assailed the West for being undemocratic has ruled Libya as a dictator for three decades, ruthlessly quashing any dissent.

On the other hand, in his 40 years in power Qaddafi has striven to improve the material quality of life for the Libyan people—and in some respects he has succeeded. Yet his unusual philosophy and frequently shifting domestic policies have contributed to a degree of chaos and economic stagnation in Libya. As Dr. Lillian Craig Harris, in her book *Libya: Qadhafi's Revolution and the Modern State*, explains: "The welfare state—with its free services, subsidized food, inexpensive housing, social security programs, and medical and educational benefits—has greatly improved the lives of the people. But Libyan society has

In 1977 Libya's governing body, the General People's Congress, adopted "Socialist People's Libyan Arab Jamahiriya" as the country's official name. Muammar Qaddafi added the word "Great" in 1986, after U.S. warplanes pounded Tripoli and Benghazi in retaliation for Libyan-sponsored acts of terrorism.

increasingly become one in which lack of incentive is rewarded and initiative, particularly of the political or economic sort, can mean trouble."

Dirk Vandewalle, author of *Libya Since Independence: Oil and State-Building*, expands on this idea. "Libya," he writes, "remains a political system where no opposition is tolerated, where arbitrariness remains the rule of politics, and where its citizens continue every day to experience deliberate, state-sponsored unpredictability. Under such conditions, broad-based and lasting economic reform is unlikely to succeed."

LIBYA AND THE WORLD

If the policies of Muammar Qaddafi have caused problems domestically, they have also largely isolated Libya internationally— and even, to a certain extent, within the Arab world. Qaddafi's regime long supported an array of terrorist and revolutionary organizations from all over the world—and it was also implicated directly in several infamous terrorist attacks against Western targets.

In addition, Libya's relations with its neighbors—even fellow Arab nations—frequently turned bitter. Qaddafi funded rebels and sponsored attempts to topple the governments of neighboring countries. Libyan forces fought occasional border wars or occupied neighbors' territory. As a result, Libya became something of an international pariah.

Some observers noted an apparent shift in Libyan behavior in the last years of the 20th century and the first years of the 21st. Domestically, Libya seemed to be exhibiting a degree of openness; in foreign affairs Qaddafi's tone appeared more moderate, his sponsorship of terrorism less prevalent. Whether these represented long-term changes for Libya, or what direction the country might take in a post-Qaddafi future, remained unclear.

This photograph shows the beginnings of a ghibli windstorm near the Libya-Tunisia border. The powerful wind, which can cause dust storms and sandstorms, is one of the country's more dangerous natural features.

The Land

Imagine a dark wall that spans the horizon as far as you can see and rises hundreds of feet into the air. It is advancing quickly toward you across the desert. There is no escape. A hot, dry, powerful wind known as the *ghibli* has blown up a sandstorm, and you must take whatever cover you can find and wait for the storm to pass. Even though you close up your desert home as tightly as you can, a layer of dust will coat the interior after the sandstorm passes, a few hours—or several days—later. Even so, you are lucky: the ghibli is strong enough to blow people off their feet, and to be caught without shelter when a sandstorm whips across the Libyan desert is to court death.

Ghibli-fed sandstorms—which sweep northward from the Sahara Desert mainly in spring and early autumn but can occur at all times of the year—mark Libya as a harsh land. Yet there are other conditions that make life throughout much of this North African country a continual struggle against nature.

THE SAHARA

Libya is part of—and in a certain sense, defined by—the Sahara Desert. The world's largest and most famous desert, the Sahara spans northern Africa from the Atlantic coast to the Red Sea. The Sahara covers Libya except for a narrow coastal strip in the country's north. Throughout history, the great desert has been the scene of remarkable adventures, tragedies, and tests of endurance. People crossing the Sahara, including entire caravans, have frequently disappeared without a trace.

A common misperception is that the Sahara Desert is a wasteland of seemingly endless sand flats and dunes—a "sea of sand." In reality, the Sahara also consists of rocks and cliff-fringed highlands. The Al-Jifarah Plain in northwestern Libya, for example, rises 1,000 feet (305 meters) from the sea and spans some 10,000 square miles (25,890 square kilometers). In central Libya there are even volcanic mountains.

Even among the other Saharan nations of North Africa, however, Libya is an unusually dry land. It has no permanent rivers or lakes. Ancient riverbeds called **wadis** briefly fill with water after rare flash floods, but they quickly go dry again. The especially arid land in the south may receive no rain at all for six years at a time or longer. In large part because of this lack of water, only 1 percent of Libya's land is arable (that is, usable for farming). In fact, it's estimated that less than 5 percent of Libyan terrain is useful for agricultural *or* industrial production. Desert and semidesert areas make up 92 percent of the country, and in those areas people cluster around the occasional **oasis**—a small, isolated area where a reliable underground water source sustains plants and humans.

In Libya's desert regions, the heat can be searing. Temperatures frequently climb well above 100°F (38°C) on summer days. In fact, the highest temperature ever recorded was in Al Aziziyah in north-western Libya. In 1922 thermometers there registered 136.4°F (58°C).

THE MEDITERRANEAN COAST

Along the Mediterranean coast in Libya's far north, however, climatic conditions are much less harsh, with more moderate

The Sahara Desert is not just an ocean of sand, as shown in the top photo; salt flats (right), surrounded by rocky cliffs, are among the natural features that can be found in Libya's central Saharan region.

temperatures and seasonal precipitation. From autumn to spring, rainstorms douse the coastal regions, nourishing a variety of vegetation. Because of the more hospitable climate, about 70 percent of Libya's 6 million people live along the Mediterranean Sea.

THREE MAJOR GEOGRAPHICAL REGIONS

With a total area of 679,358 square miles (1,759,540 sq km), Libya is a fairly large nation—slightly larger than Alaska and Minnesota combined. It is basically square in shape, with a pointed dip in the southeast. Measuring approximately 930 miles (1,497 km) from the southern tip to the northern coast, and about 1,050 miles (1,690 km) from east to west, Libya has a coastline of approximately 1,100 miles (1,770 km). Geographically, Libya consists of three principal regions: Tripolitania, Cyrenaica, and Fezzan.

A fruit orchard in Libya. Only about 2 percent of the country is arable land, found mostly in the Jebel Akhdar region near Benghazi, and the Al-Jifarah Plain, near Tripoli.

Tripolitania, located in northwestern Libya, contains the country's largest city, economic heart, and political capital—Tripoli, which lies along the Mediterranean coast about 100 miles (161 km) from the Tunisian border. Tripolitania also contains a portion of the country's very limited fertile land, where farmers grow grain, vegetables, and fruits.

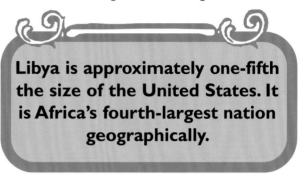

Libya is approximately one-fifth the size of the United States. It is Africa's fourth-largest nation geographically.

Near the Mediterranean shoreline are marshes and grasslands. Yet the desert isn't far away. Moving eastward along the large Gulf of Sidra in north-central Libya, the Mediterranean surf laps dry, barren terrain for some 300 miles (483 km). This finger of desert geographically separates the region of Tripolitania from the region of Cyrenaica.

Like Tripolitania to the west, the eastern region of Cyrenaica contains arable territory near the Mediterranean shore, and desert in the south. Cyrenaica is also the home of Libya's Green Mountains. This low range is covered with flowers, juniper trees, and scrub plants.

South of Tripolitania and Cyrenaica lies Libya's third major geographical region: Fezzan. A desert region of sand dunes, gravel, and stones, Fezzan displays the full panorama of the formidable Saharan landscape. Human activity here is generally confined to oasis settlements, though intrepid caravanners still ply the sands on camelback, much as did traders of old.

In many respects, the nation now known as Libya and made up of the geographical regions of Tripolitania, Cyrenaica, and Fezzan is an artificial—and a European—invention. Until the European powers "partitioned" Africa and began colonizing different areas of the continent during the late 1800s, most of the official boundary lines that define modern African nations did not exist. People living within the area of today's Libya would not have considered themselves Libyans as distinct from, say, Algerians or Tunisians. Desert **nomads** had little conception of national boundaries as they wandered the region in search of water and forage for their livestock. And the regions of Tripolitania, Cyrenaica, and Fezzan were in many ways separate lands unto themselves well into the era of independence. As late as the mid-20th century a traveler might tell friends she or he was planning a trip "to Tripolitania" or "to Tripoli"—not "to Libya."

Historically, some of the peoples of Tripolitania had close social and economic ties with what is now Tunisia. Peoples of ancient Cyrenaica had bonds with what is today western Egypt. In the south, residents of the Fezzan region held much in common with the peoples of present-day northern Chad and Niger.

In the broader Arab world, Tripolitania was considered part of the **Maghreb**, which encompassed what is now northwestern Libya, Tunisia, Algeria, and, far to the west, Morocco. Cyrenaica and neighboring Egypt were part of the eastern Arab domain, known as the **Mashriq**. The people of Fezzan were basically aligned with neither the Maghreb nor the Mashriq; for practical purposes, they paid homage only to the tribes in control of the oases on which their lives depended.

TOPOGRAPHY

Overall, Libya is a relatively flat country. Modest highland plateaus, or tablelands, are seen near the coast and in the far south. In addition to the Al-Jifarah Plain in the northwest, highlighted by the Nafusah Plateau, the limestone Akhdar Mountains extend approximately 100 miles (161 km) along the northeastern coast, rising 2,000 to 3,000 feet (610 to 915 meters). Bikku Bitti, the country's highest peak, rises to 7,434 feet (2,267 meters) in the

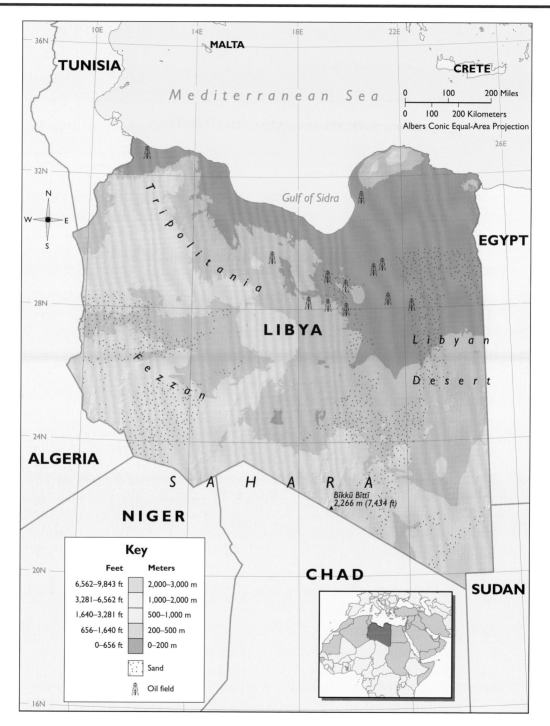

As this map shows, much of Libya's interior is sandy or rocky desert. The country's largest oil fields, Defa-Wafa and Nasser, are located in the north-central region.

Tibesti mountain range at the Chad border in the south.

ANIMAL AND PLANT LIFE

While the Libyan desert is a hostile environment for humans and most plants and animals, it is not altogether a lifeless waste. Insects, lizards, snakes, rodents, and even larger animals such as foxes and antelopes make the Sahara their home. They are rarely seen by day, when they must take cover from the scorching sun—

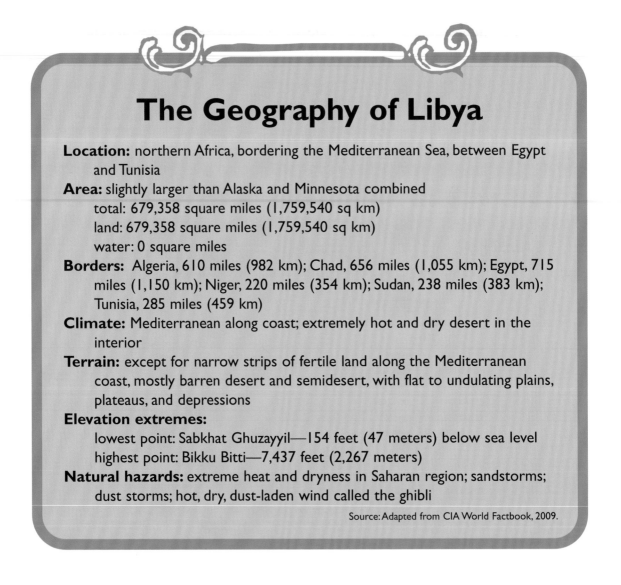

The Geography of Libya

Location: northern Africa, bordering the Mediterranean Sea, between Egypt and Tunisia

Area: slightly larger than Alaska and Minnesota combined
  total: 679,358 square miles (1,759,540 sq km)
  land: 679,358 square miles (1,759,540 sq km)
  water: 0 square miles

Borders: Algeria, 610 miles (982 km); Chad, 656 miles (1,055 km); Egypt, 715 miles (1,150 km); Niger, 220 miles (354 km); Sudan, 238 miles (383 km); Tunisia, 285 miles (459 km)

Climate: Mediterranean along coast; extremely hot and dry desert in the interior

Terrain: except for narrow strips of fertile land along the Mediterranean coast, mostly barren desert and semidesert, with flat to undulating plains, plateaus, and depressions

Elevation extremes:
  lowest point: Sabkhat Ghuzayyil—154 feet (47 meters) below sea level
  highest point: Bikku Bitti—7,437 feet (2,267 meters)

Natural hazards: extreme heat and dryness in Saharan region; sandstorms; dust storms; hot, dry, dust-laden wind called the ghibli

Source: Adapted from CIA World Factbook, 2009.

many by burrowing into the sand. At night, however, the desert comes alive as they emerge to feed in the cool (and at times chilly) air.

The male gazelle, called the *waddan*, is Libya's national animal. Birds of Libya range from larks, prairie hens, and partridges to owls, hawks, eagles, and vultures. Snakes, some of them poisonous, and other reptiles can be seen in the oases.

In the north, along the Mediterranean coast, rain nourishes several varieties of grasses, herbs, juniper and lentisk (mastic tree) forests, and other vegetation. In the main, Libya is bare of forestland, but after independence in 1951 the government sponsored the planting of millions of acres of cypress, cedar, eucalyptus, and other trees in the Tripolitania region.

As one travels south, plant life becomes increasingly less abundant. In some areas, hardy grasses rise during rainy periods. In desert oases, date palms and a few flowers provide a pleasant contrast to the barren surrounding landscape. Henna, a shrub used to produce a red dye, also grows in oases, as do pistachio trees, which yield a tasty nut. Appropriately enough for a country that consists mostly of desert, however, Libya's national plant is the cactus.

Tourists walk under the Severan arch in Leptis Magna, which was built around A.D. 203. Libya's fascinating history dates back thousands of years. The original Berber settlers in the region were influenced by the arrival of other cultures—the Phoenicians, the Romans, and, most significantly, the Arabs, who spread the Islamic faith into North Africa.

History

Among the earliest inhabitants of Libya were the Berbers, nomadic peoples believed to have been living in North Africa at least 5,000 years ago. Historians aren't sure where the Berbers originated; many may have come from Asia and intermingled with other peoples from around the Mediterranean Basin.

By 2000 B.C., the Berbers were establishing settlements along the Mediterranean coast and in the Saharan oases. Where the land was fertile, they grew crops. Elsewhere, they wandered with their herds, seeking fresh pastures and water sources. The Berbers spoke different dialects (variations on a common language), and they were organized by family and clan, not as a united people. They traditionally have considered themselves *imazighan*—"free men."

In their quest for new lands to farm and graze, some of the Berbers infringed on early Egyptian civilization in the fertile

This cave art showing a deer-like animal, found in the mountainous region of Tadrart Acacus, in the Libyan Sahara, may have been created around 12,000 B.C. Tadrart Acacus is located near Libya's southwestern border with Algeria, east of the city of Ghat. Tools, carvings, and cave paintings found throughout the mountains reflect the cultures of the various peoples who lived in Libya before recorded history.

Nile River delta. Rather than drive them away, the powerful Egyptians became their masters, forcing the Berbers to pay **tribute** to the Egyptian **pharaoh**. Some of these eastern Berbers became soldiers in the Egyptian army; others, trusted officers in the pharaoh's government. Around 950 B.C., one Berber official became so influential that he took control of the Egyptian kingdom, becoming pharaoh and beginning a period of "Libyan dynasties" in Egypt that lasted two centuries.

THE PHOENICIANS AND THE GREEKS

Visitors from other continents began arriving around 1000 B.C. First came the Phoenicians, seafaring traders from the eastern Mediterranean coast. The Phoenicians began to exchange goods with Berber tribes and to build commercial outposts along the North African shoreline. Their most famous North African port city, Carthage, was located in what is today Tunisia. The Phoenicians also built trading centers in northwestern Libya at the sites of modern-day Sabratha, Tripoli, and Leptis Magna. Through these strategic cities passed gold, ivory, exotic bird feathers, and other trade goods brought up from the African interior. These products ultimately turned up in Asian and European cities.

Phoenician civilization along the Mediterranean coast of North Africa is known to history as "Punic" civilization. Carthage and other Phoenician settlements in the region would battle ancient Rome for supremacy in the western Mediterranean in a series of conflicts beginning in the third century B.C. Ultimately Rome prevailed in those conflicts, which historians call the Punic Wars.

A few centuries after the Phoenicians arrived in North Africa, the Greeks began expanding their influence around the Mediterranean. Greeks established a colony in northeastern Libya (now the region of Cyrenaica) with its capital at the port of Cyrene. Founded in 631 B.C., Cyrene became a thriving center of production, trade, and learning. To the ancient Greeks—like the Phoenicians before them and conquerors who would come later—the region that is now coastal Libya was important as a food source. At one point, Greek ships transported great stores of food across the sea from Libya to relieve the city of Athens during a famine. Cyrenaica was noted for its grain, livestock, and wine. The region also provided wool for clothing, and the Greeks were intrigued by exotic, mysterious Cyrenaican herbs, which they believed improved their health.

During the Phoenician and Greek period in coastal Libya, the oases in Fezzan—the desert region south of Tripolitania—were under the control of a powerful tribal group, the Garamentes. Their capital was at Germa, some 400 miles (644 km) from the Mediterranean. Much of the network of North African caravan routes, both north-south and east-west, passed through the land of the Garamentes. Besides influencing trade, the Garamentes were resourceful builders, farmers, and livestock breeders. They developed a sophisticated underground irrigation system and built thousands of small pyramids.

THE ROMAN ERA

During the second and first centuries B.C., the Romans succeeded the Greeks in dominance of the Mediterranean. They sacked Carthage in 146 B.C. and invaded the region of northern Libya. Tripolitania and Cyrenaica became Roman provinces.

The Romans coveted North Africa not simply for its strategic importance but also for its fertile coastal strips, which were productive grain-growing areas. Two thousand years ago, northern Africa had a more humid climate and more territory suitable for agriculture. Tripolitania was especially important to Rome for its production of olive oil. In addition, from this province were shipped many of the slaves and much of the gold brought northward from the African interior.

Roman legions did not probe deeply into the Sahara. Rome was interested mainly in the natural and trade resources of the coastal areas, which could be controlled with relative ease. The Romans maintained forces strong enough to protect their North African holdings from marauding desert bands, and eventually they established friendly trade with the Garamentes in the Fezzan region.

However, they saw little reason to attempt military dominance over the desert—an undertaking that offered slim prospects of lasting success and, in any event, would have been extremely costly.

In the late fourth century A.D., the vast Roman Empire split into western and eastern halves. A century later, the Western Roman Empire collapsed, in part because of military pressures from various barbarian tribes, among them the Vandals. Fierce warriors from central Europe, the Vandals eventually overran the whole Mediterranean realm, from Spain all the way to northern Africa.

The great Carthaginian general Hannibal Barca battles the Roman army in this painting of a scene from the Second Punic War; the soldiers from Carthage are mounted on war elephants. The Punic Wars were a series of conflicts between the two major powers of the time, Rome and Carthage. The first lasted from 264 to 241 B.C., and the second began in 218 B.C. and ended a year after Hannibal's defeat at the Battle of Zama in 202. After the Third Punic War (149–146 B.C.), Roman legions totally destroyed the city of Carthage and took control of its former provinces in North Africa.

Their influence in Libya was comparatively short-lived. In 535, forces of the Eastern Roman, or Byzantine, Empire—which was centered in Constantinople (modern-day Istanbul, Turkey)—conquered the Vandals in northern Africa. Byzantine occupation would also prove short-lived, however.

THE COMING OF THE ARABS

In the seventh century, Arab armies fighting under the banner of their new religion, Islam, emerged from the Arabian Peninsula and swept across the lower Mediterranean coast. By 642 they had invaded Cyrenaica; by the next year, Tripolitania. In a few years they held control of Germa, the remote desert capital of the Garamentes in the Fezzan region. Within a century they had pressed to the northwestern shoulder of the African continent (modern-day Morocco) and had even invaded the Spanish peninsula at the upper entrance to the Mediterranean. Various Berber and Arab Muslim dynasties controlled North Africa for the next 900 years.

Initially the Arabs were harsh conquerors. They ravaged and plundered North African towns and farms, attacked caravans, and slew anyone who opposed them—as well as some who didn't. In the face of the onslaught, many Berber tribes fled into the heart of the desert and the arid mountains. From there, small bands of guerrilla fighters periodically emerged to lash back at the Arabs. Eventually, though, the Arabs quashed Berber resistance.

At the same time, many Berbers converted to Islam and fought with the Arabs in their relentless military campaigns. Over the following centuries, under the rule of various Islamic dynasties, Berbers and Arabs intermingled in North Africa to varying degrees. In Morocco and Algeria, Berber languages and cultures have been preserved right up until the present day by a significant portion of the population. In Libya and Tunisia, on the other hand, most Berbers were eventually Arabized.

THE OTTOMANS TAKE OVER

At the end of the 14th century, a new dynasty arose in Asia Minor that would have a decisive impact on the entire Middle East and North Africa for hundreds of years. In 1453 the Ottomans—Muslims but Turks rather than Arabs—captured Constantinople and made it their capital. From there the Ottoman Empire would push northward to the Balkan territories and around the Mediterranean, across northern Africa.

In 1551 an Ottoman naval force commanded by Admiral Sinan **Pasha** took control of Tripoli from Spanish forces, who had occupied the city for 40 years. Soon practically the whole of modern-day Libya fell under Ottoman rule. Shrewd administrators, the Ottomans realized that they could never directly rule all of their vast domain. So they left practical control of day-to-day affairs in the hands of local leaders.

The Ottomans divided the Maghreb (their western Arab domain) into three parts, with governments at Tripoli, Algiers, and Tunis. A pasha, or governor, was appointed in Tripoli. At his disposal was a military force of **janissaries**, peasants from Turkey who became elite professional soldiers. By the 1600s the janissary commanders exercised more actual power in Tripolitania than did the pasha. Suleiman Safar, the janissaries' overall commander, effectively became the province's government leader in 1611. During the next century, a steady succession of military leaders seized power temporarily, only to be ousted—often in a savage bloodbath—by another ambitious army commander.

Stable, though brutal, leadership came in 1711 when a cavalry officer named Ahmad Karamanli took control of Tripoli. Popular with the military forces, he was able to remain in power more than 30 years. Karamanli (also spelled Qaramanli) formally recognized the authority of the Ottomans but generally governed as he pleased.

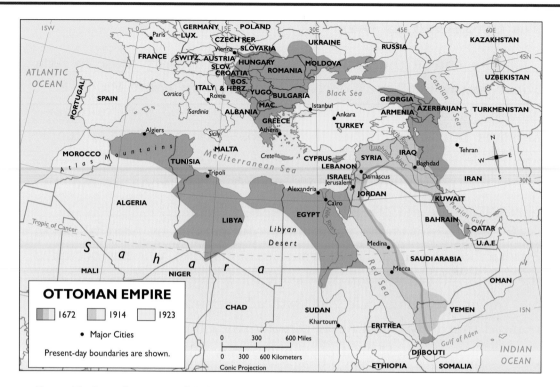

From Turkey, the powerful Ottoman Empire spread throughout the Middle East during the 15th and 16th centuries. By 1672 the empire controlled large parts of North Africa, as well as much of the rest of the Middle East, central Asia, and eastern Europe. By the start of World War I (1914), however, the Ottomans had been forced out of North Africa.

Partly through trade with European countries and partly through piracy, he acquired considerable wealth. Eventually, he exerted control over part of Cyrenaica as well. He established a hereditary line of leaders who continued the Karamanli legacy throughout most of the 18th century.

His successors were not nearly as effective in governing the region. Ali Benghul, a Turkish army officer, led a **coup** in 1793 that interrupted the Karamanli era and briefly returned the Ottomans to actual authority in Tripoli. Two years later, however, Yusuf ibn Ali Karamanli seized control and made himself pasha. Yusuf ruled until 1832. During this time, he built a formidable military force. His army included professional soldiers, slaves, and, on occasion, tribal warriors who were enticed to fight for Yusuf in return for looting privileges.

THE BARBARY PIRATES

Yusuf's navy was regarded by Europeans and Americans as little better than a coalition of pirates who had the blessing of their government. Through the centuries North African seaports had acquired an unsavory reputation as pirate lairs. In fact, in ancient times Phoenician commanders had pressed Berbers into service as pirate crews and raided foreign shipping across the Mediterranean, using Tripoli and other ports as their bases.

At the end of the 18th century, in its early years as an independent country, the United States had virtually no navy. As a result, American merchant ships were unprotected. American vessels trading in Mediterranean ports fell prey to pirates operating along what was known as the Barbary Coast—the area of North Africa extending eastward from Morocco on the Atlantic, almost to Egypt. Barbary pirates, who were known as **corsairs**, commandeered the merchant ships. For a price, the Barbary governments offered to return the captured vessels and the people aboard.

Americans were outraged, but the United States was initially powerless to stop the corsairs. Rather, it paid a tribute to the North African rulers in return for free passage through their waters. America paid Yusuf's regime in Tripoli $18,000 annually—an enormous sum then that would equal more than a million dollars in today's currency. To Pasha Yusuf, the policy of demanding tribute was only fair. He viewed it as little different from other countries' practice of imposing shipping and trade taxes on foreign goods and products entering their ports. Maritime taxes were important sources of revenue for many governments. In the case of the Mediterranean raiders, however, international anger was aroused because the pirates sometimes sold captured crewmen and passengers into slavery.

In the early 1800s, when Yusuf demanded increasing tribute from foreign seafaring powers, America with its new navy challenged the Barbary corsairs. These actions, coupled with international pressures and military campaigns against pirate lairs by European naval powers, ultimately forced Tripoli and the other Barbary states to stop their demands for tribute.

FOREIGN INTERVENTIONS

The Tripoli government owed money to France and Great Britain, and it had come to rely on foreign tribute to keep its economy balanced. When payment of that tribute ended, Tripoli could not afford to import basic necessities or pay its debts to foreign governments. To make up for the loss of income, the Tripoli regime levied heavy

taxes on its own people. This prompted revolts among the tribes and, ultimately, civil war. Pasha Yusuf, understanding the gravity of the situation, gave up his leadership in 1832. His son Ali II reigned for the next three troubled years. Unhappily for Ali II, he made the mistake of requesting Ottoman assistance, hoping to prevent the European powers from claiming dominion over Tripoli to satisfy the debts owed them. Obligingly, the Ottomans sent a Turkish army to establish order in the face of Tripoli's internal violence. But the Turks took the occasion to oust Ali from power and send him into exile. Once again, Tripolitania was an Ottoman province.

In 1835 the high Ottoman rulers in Istanbul began exerting direct control over the region. Turks held the principal government offices, although they accepted advice from traditional tribal leaders of the region. The Ottomans never effectively controlled the interior, however—nor did they really try. In 1879 the Ottomans made Cyrenaica a province separate from Tripolitania.

Turkish administrators were in control until 1911. In autumn of that year, Italy accused Turkey of encouraging tribal hostility against Italian interests in Libya. Italy had been eager to establish a colony in North Africa, where England, France, and other European powers already exerted control. Tripoli, due south across the

This 19th-century drawing shows ships of the U.S. Navy bombarding coastal fortifications in Tripoli. From bases on the coast of North Africa the Barbary pirates had raided Mediterranean shipping for centuries. Other countries were forced to pay tribute to keep their ships from being attacked. When the United States refused in May 1801, Pasha Yusuf of Tripolitania declared war. However, the U.S. Navy was up to the challenge; by 1805 American marines had captured Tripoli and eradicated the strongholds of the Barbary pirates.

Mediterranean only 350 miles (563 km) from Italy's southern tip, was the most logical area for the Italians to attempt to colonize.

Declaring war against Turkey, Italy easily captured Tripoli, Benghazi, Tobruk, Darnah, and other Libyan coastal cities. The following year Turkey, preoccupied with greater military threats elsewhere, agreed to withdraw from Tripoli and Cyrenaica, leaving those regions "independent"—but knowing that Italy was prepared to claim them as overseas territories. Thus, Libya in effect became an Italian colony in October 1912. It would remain so until World War II.

From beginning to end, Libyans in different areas resisted the Italian presence. **Bedouin** tribes of the desert ignored the Italians' claims over their territory. They and other groups waged ongoing warfare against these new invaders, and Italy never effectively controlled the broad desert country. In the Cyrenaica region, the powerful Sanusi order of Muslims spearheaded resistance. In 1914 and 1915, the Sanusis spread their opposition campaign into the Fezzan region and elsewhere—even thrusting into Tripolitania. Their actions were so widespread and determined that the campaign would be remembered in history as the First Italo-Sanusi War.

Italy, meanwhile, was caught up in World War I. Germany and Turkey, Italy's enemies in the world conflict, supplied weapons and military officers to the Sanusis in Libya.

The Sanusis soon overreached themselves, however. Led by Turkish commanders, a Sanusi force in 1916 invaded neighboring Egypt. There the British, allies of Italy, crushed them. The Sanusi leader, Ahmad ash Sharif, fled to Turkey. His young cousin, Muhammad Idris al Mahdi as-Sanusi, became the leader of Cyrenaica. Idris was friendly toward the British—though not toward their Italian allies. He agreed to a truce until World War I ended in Europe.

While Italy was held in low esteem by the Libyan people, it was in a strong position internationally after the war, as one of the victorious Allied nations. The European powers thus recognized

Italy's colonial claims in North Africa. But the Italians found that actually establishing their authority there was no easier after the war than it had been in 1912. In some towns, they were virtually surrounded by hostile tribesmen. Beyond a narrow coastal zone, Italian influence was negligible.

In order to forge a workable relationship with the intractable local population they claimed to rule, the Italians gave them a degree of control. They let the inhabitants have provincial legislatures, and they appointed native advisers in different locales. They divided their North African holdings. At this point in history, there was no "Libya" as we know it today. Tripolitania and Cyrenaica were separate Italian colonies. The sparsely populated Fezzan region, whose natural features for centuries had defied the very idea of colonization, became a sort of Italian military district.

In Cyrenaica, where Idris and the Sanusis posed especially

Italian forces capture Benghazi during the Italo-Turkish War. The fighting began in September 1911, and the Italian army soon occupied Tripoli, Derna, and Benghazi. However, because of stiff resistance the Italians concentrated their operations on the coastal areas. Ultimately, Italy succeeded in its goal of gaining colonies in North Africa. On October 18, 1912, Turkey signed the Treaty of Lausanne, which conceded the Ottoman provinces of Tripolitania and Cyrenaica to Italy.

powerful opposition, Italy was obliged to accept Idris's regime as official. Idris became the tribal **emir** of the province. Unlike the many puppet officials European colonialists handpicked in other parts of Africa, Idris had real power. The Italians gave him independent authority over a vast interior domain that included important oases. Sanusi leaders were appointed to the provincial parliament. The Sanusi army was merged into the Italian occupation force.

MURMURS OF NATIONALISM—AND WAR

By this time, the first political movements were afoot for an independent Libya. In the Tripolitanian port of Misratah, a group of political activists seeking an Arab union met in 1919. They demanded that Italy recognize the whole area's independence, but their efforts fell apart amid internal disagreements. The next year, another assembly proclaimed the independent "nation" of Tripolitania. But this, too, failed to gain widespread support among the people.

Disunity among the Libyan factions was largely to blame. Nationalist leaders in Tripolitania were unfriendly toward the Sanusis of Cyrenaica. Meanwhile, many tribal peoples in other parts of the territory were simply not interested in taking up arms to create an independent nation—though they would fight for the freedom to continue the way of life of their ancestors, and they viewed the Italian occupation as a challenge to Islam.

During the last 3,000 years, a number of foreign powers have conquered what is today northern Libya—and in turn have been driven out or have merged with the ancient Berber civilization. They have included Phoenicians, Romans, Arabs, Turks, and Italians.

In 1922 nationalist leaders from Tripolitania and Cyrenaica met to discuss united opposition to Italian dominion. Although people in the two regions had serious differences, the Tripolitanians proposed an alliance. Surprisingly, they agreed to let Idris rule as emir of the combined provinces. After long deliberation, Idris reluctantly accepted the proposal.

Predictably, the Italian government was alarmed. Unwilling to risk war with Italy, Idris fled to neighboring Egypt in 1923. In time, he would return to his homeland and reclaim his role as leader of a united Libya.

The departure of Idris did not prevent war. While he was agonizing over whether to accept rulership over the combined domain, Benito Mussolini became dictator of Italy. Mussolini believed Libya must be brought under control by force. The Second Italo-Sanusi War began when Italian soldiers occupied Benghazi, Cyrenaica's important port city. The Sanusis took up arms, led by Umar al-Mukhtar. Throughout the 1920s, ragtag Sanusi tribal bands waged a guerrilla war, attacking Italian army units and cutting telegraph lines. The problem for the Italians was finding the enemy and engaging in pitched battle. After inflicting their damage, the Sanusi raiders would vanish into the desert.

Brutal retaliation came in the years 1929 to 1931, however. Italian commander Rudolfo Graziani sent tank and artillery columns into the desert to find and destroy the marauders' hideouts. The Italians were supported by a new military weapon the Sanusis could not counter: the airplane. The Italian army filled in vital desert wells, forced tribal peoples into concentration camps, and killed the animals that supplied al-Mukhtar's guerrilla fighters with food. Sanusi opposition weakened. The war effectively ended when al-Mukhtar was caught and executed in 1931.

It has been estimated that during the colonial era, at least 750,000 Libyans fled to other countries or died in their struggle against the Italian occupiers. As a result, the native population did not increase significantly between 1911 and 1950.

One segment of the population did grow dramatically, however:

Italian immigrants. A major objective of Italy's African colonization was to encourage Italian nationals to settle there, thus relieving overcrowding in Italy. During the 1920s, 1930s, and early 1940s, more than 100,000 Italians settled in Libya, which Mussolini called Italy's "Fourth Shore." As an incentive to them, Italy's Fascist government made major improvements in Libya's farming and transportation systems.

German tanks race across the Libyan desert, 1942. During World War II, North Africa was a key battleground, controlled early by the Axis powers Germany and Italy. In June 1942 the German general Erwin Rommel won a major tank battle at Tobruk, Libya, on his way to Egypt, where he hoped to capture the strategically important Suez Canal. In October, however, Rommel's advance was stopped at El Alamein by an Allied force commanded by General Bernard Montgomery.

During the 1930s, Italy began using the name "Libya" to refer to its North African coastal colony. It did not include the Fezzan region, which the Italians called "South Tripolitania" and regarded as simply a military zone. An Italian governor oversaw the colony, and Italians held all the important government posts. Tribal leaders had little power beyond their limited spheres of influence.

The Italian administration gave some of the ancient Bedouin grazing lands to Italian farmers. While improving the lot of Italian settlers, the colonial government did little for the original inhabitants. Most of the living improvements realized by the natives—sanitation projects and medical care, for example—resulted from Italy's eagerness to lure Italian nationals to the colony. While colonial administrations in other parts of Africa saw that basic schooling was provided for native children (by missionaries, in many cases), Italy provided no education for non-Italian Libyans.

World War II (1939–45) destroyed Italy's colonial scheme. In North Africa, Italy joined its ally Germany in fighting against British, Free French, and U.S. forces. At first, German and Italian forces controlled the North African sands. By 1943, however, British and American tank divisions had gained the upper hand. They were aided by Sanusi volunteers from among the Libyan people.

War-torn Libya was hardly a tenable land for the thousands of Italian settlers, who crossed the Mediterranean Sea en masse to return to Italy. By war's end, Libya was largely free from European rule. But it was left with ruined cities, a ravaged economy, and an impoverished, poorly educated population split by regional and political differences.

THE REIGN OF KING IDRIS

For four years after the war, the United Nations debated what should become of decimated Libya. In the end, the international community opted for a kingdom independent of outside rule. A

Libyan national assembly selected the country's first king, Idris I, in 1950. Idris—who had emerged as leader of the Sanusis in Cyrenaica during World War I—was granted total authority, unchallenged by political parties. This form of government is known as a **monarchy**. Independence for Libya was officially declared on December 24, 1951.

King Idris at the time was a national hero. Many Libyans considered him their rightful leader, restored to power after years of unjust exile. His family heirs were designated his successors as king. But to ensure his hold on power, Idris banned political opposition and sent the most worrisome rival leader into exile. He even scattered his own relatives, fearing possible revolt.

For the most part, Idris was friendly toward Western governments. He allowed Great Britain and the United States to establish military bases in Libya. This not only brought in "rent" revenue but also provided the fledgling nation with a degree of international security. Later, when oil was discovered in Libya, foreign petroleum companies were needed to provide the technology and expertise to develop Libya's new boom industry.

However, Libya did not become a puppet or even a firm ally of the Western nations. It joined the Arab League in 1953 and forged diplomatic relations with the Soviet Union two years later. King Idris refused to allow Great Britain to land soldiers in Libya during the 1956 Suez Canal crisis, precipitated by Egypt's seizure of the British- and French-owned canal that cut through its territory. Idris was not inclined to help Western powers in conflicts against other Arab nations.

Nevertheless, many inside his own country considered King Idris to be too pro-Western. Another growing source of discontent was regional tension. Many people in Tripolitania were displeased with having a Sanusi ruler from Cyrenaica. Disputes between regional government officials became so serious that Idris's regime agreed to let Tripoli and Benghazi alternate as Libya's capital city—Tripoli in winter and Benghazi in summer.

After oil exports began in the early 1960s, Libyans noticed that the petroleum revenues were making Idris and his supporters wealthier but were hardly improving the lot of the average citizen. While members of Idris's family and government reveled in the good life, the general populace languished in poverty and became increasingly discontent. By the late 1960s, the country was ripe for a radical change in leadership. A number of factions within the Libyan military, the business community, and even the royal establishment were poised for an opportunity to seize power.

King Idris (1890–1983) works at a desk in 1952, shortly after the declaration of Libya's independence. Idris had been a Libyan nationalist for many years, but had been forced to flee the country by Italian officials. During World War II, Idris led the Libyan Arab Force, which fought with the American, British, and Free French armies in North Africa. After becoming king in 1951, Idris ruled until 1969, when his government was overthrown in a bloodless coup. He lived the rest of his life in exile in Egypt.

QADDAFI'S COUP

The king's lavish lifestyle and his political balancing act—cooperation with the Arab world while retaining close ties with the West—caught up with him on September 1, 1969. While Idris was out of the country obtaining medical treatment, a group of military men calling themselves the Free Unionist Officers, climaxing years of planning and waiting, seized control of the government with comparative ease. King Idris publicly abdicated his thrown, pledging not to oppose the coup. He retired to an exile in Egypt, where he died in 1983.

Libyan leader Muammar al-Qaddafi speaks with Jordan's King Abdullah in Tripoli. Although Qaddafi has been a confrontational leader for more than 30 years, in the Arab world he has gained a measure of respect.

One week after the 1969 coup, Captain Muammar al-Qaddafi, just 27 years old, emerged as the country's new leader. He was promoted to colonel and declared commander-in-chief of the Libyan military. Inspired by the **pan-Arab** ideology of Egyptian leader Gamal Abdel Nasser, Qaddafi scorned European and American involvement in his country's oil industry. His regime pledged three ideals for the new Libya: "freedom, socialism, and unity."

Three decades later, at the beginning of the 21st century, Qaddafi still controlled Libya—though by then he had given up any official title. Under his strict and—to Western observers at least—often bizarre leadership, Libya underwent dramatic political, social, and economic changes.

Using the country's oil wealth, Qaddafi supported military coups and terrorism in other countries. He claimed that Libya was making progress on development of a nuclear weapons program. By 1992 Libya had been politically isolated from the rest of the world by UN and U.S. government sanctions. In 2001 the U.S. government labeled Libya as a state sponsor of terrorism.

But beginning in the 1990s Qaddafi began rebuilding relations with Western nations. During the first decade of the 21st century, he worked to restore diplomatic and trade ties with European countries and the United States. Although still considered an unpredictable leader today, Qaddafi continues to demonstrate the political shrewdness that has kept him in power for decades—and made him the longest-serving leader in the Arab world.

A Libyan missile mounted on a vehicle passes in front of a mosque in Tripoli during a military parade marking the 30th anniversary of the Libyan Revolution that brought Muammar al-Qaddafi to power, September 1, 1999.

Politics, the Economy, and Religion

Libyan politics for the past three decades can be summarized in a single word: Qaddafi. After coming to power in a coup in 1969, he quickly demonstrated a forceful, uncompromising brand of leadership. One of his government's first acts was to confiscate the homes and property of many longtime residents of foreign lineage—with the result that most of them left Libya. Since then he has consistently charted his own course—often to the consternation of the international community and at significant cost to his fellow Libyans.

QADDAFI'S EARLY YEARS

A charismatic and complex figure, Muammar al-Qaddafi is descended from a family of Berber nomads near Sirte (or Sirta) in north-central Libya. He was born in a tent in 1942, herded livestock as a child, and even as Libya's leader has periodically retreated to the desert for solitude. Several of his relatives were imprisoned or killed in their fight against Italian forces during the colonial period.

Even today, many Libyans remember the hardships of the colonial era, and some historians believe that Qaddafi's disdain for Western Europe and America is rooted in the legacy of Italy's cruel colonial dominion. But Qaddafi also has expressed ire toward other foreign countries for their negative influences on Libya throughout history. For example, he has criticized Turkey for allowing Italy to take control of Libya in 1912. He has demanded that Great Britain and Italy pay Libya for damages caused by the North African military campaign of World War II.

As early as his high school years, Qaddafi actively tried to organize students to oust King Idris—and was expelled from school because of it. In spite of his interrupted studies, he obtained a law degree. Then he joined the army and immediately began to cultivate a revolutionary group of military followers.

LIBYA UNDER THE COLONEL

When Libya became a major supplier of oil to the world market in the early 1960s, King Idris used some of the new income to improve his country's educational and transportation systems. However, the king also skimmed funds for personal projects and pleasures. For that reason, Qaddafi enjoyed wide popular support when he seized power in 1969. Libyans believed he could end the corruption of the Idris regime and bring the country's different factions together.

Colonel Qaddafi responded by authorizing the construction of new hospitals, schools, and housing and undertaking desert irrigation and highway improvement projects. Clearly he was using petroleum revenues to improve living conditions in his own country. But, like Idris, he spent a portion of the oil money on other things—though no one has accused him of being attached to a lavish lifestyle. Rather, Qaddafi contributed funds and weapons to various revolutionary movements and terrorist organizations. These included traditional recipients of Arab and Islamic support, such as the Palestine Liberation Organization, but also a diverse and somewhat bewildering array of groups with few apparent ideological connections: Basque separatists in Spain, the Irish Republican Army in Northern Ireland, Japanese and Philippine revolutionaries, to name but a few. In addition, Libya was directly implicated in several incidents of international terrorism against U.S. and Western interests, including the 1986 bombing of a discotheque in

The nose section of Pan Am Flight 103 lies in wreckage, December 21, 1988. The aircraft exploded over Lockerbie, Scotland, killing all 259 passengers and crew members and 11 people on the ground. A Libyan with connections to the government's intelligence agency was later convicted in the deadly bombing.

United Nations secretary general Kofi Annan addresses a meeting of the African Union, an intergovernmental organization of African states. During the 1990s Qaddafi argued for the establishment of the AU, which was launched in 2002.

Germany frequented by American servicemen, and the bombing of a Pan Am jetliner over Lockerbie, Scotland, in 1988.

At home, Qaddafi and his agents struck fear into the hearts of Libyans who dared question his rule. Intellectuals quickly learned that those who expressed their views openly did so at their own risk, for the new leader demanded agreement with his philosophy and policies. As a result, many of Libya's best minds left the country. Even overseas, they weren't totally safe, as Libyan intelligence agents participated in the murders of Qaddafi opponents. Rival leaders within Libya were frequently jailed or assassinated. The threat of opposition to Qaddafi's regime was real: over the years, more than a dozen unsuccessful coup attempts have been made against him, most notably during the middle and late 1970s.

But not all internal measures have been directed toward maintaining Qaddafi's political control. Qaddafi also has emphasized a social and religious agenda, aspects of which Western observers have found particularly chilling. For example, his "cultural revolution" of 1973 among other things called for "appropriate measures" against individuals Qaddafi deemed to be "perverts and deviationists." He wanted to eliminate "feeble minds" from Libyan society. He also banned what he called "imported poisonous ideas."

Almost all observers acknowledge Qaddafi's skill at monitoring and shaping public opinion to maintain his popularity. One example: In 1988, he ordered hundreds of prisoners, including political opponents, freed from a Tripoli jail. He depicted himself as a forgiving leader, willing to pardon even those who had threatened his leadership and his very life.

GOVERNMENT

Thanks to his ruthlessness in suppressing dissent and his role as supreme commander of the Libyan armed forces—a heavily funded and, in comparison with the militaries of other African nations, professional force—Muammar Qaddafi is the unquestioned leader of Libya. Curiously, however, he is not officially the country's head of state. In the Great Socialist People's Libyan Arab Jamahiriya—a "government of the masses"—"the people" supposedly rule themselves without a head.

Qaddafi outlined his eclectic vision of the ideal government, which combines elements of socialism with Islamic teachings, in *The Green Book*, a tract he wrote in the 1970s. In it, he rejected Western-style representative governments. "The most tyrannical dictatorships the world has known," he maintained, "have existed under the shadow of parliaments." This, he said, is because such governments "falsify genuine democracy," which in his view is incompatible with "the electing of only a few representatives to act on behalf of great masses." Rather, he claimed, "the whole authority must be the people's."

But though Qaddafi rejected the "false democracies" of the West, neither did he endorse communism—a rival system that, its advocates claimed, ultimately leads to the withering away of the state and the equality of all citizens. Religion was at the heart of Qaddafi's objections: atheism and communism went hand in hand in the Soviet bloc, China, and other communist countries, and Qaddafi's vision of the ideal society included Islam. Shortly after seizing power in 1969, for example, he made **Sharia**, the law of Islam, the basis of his country's legal system.

Instead of embracing either of the 20th century's major competing political and economic systems, Qaddafi claimed to forge a third way. He called it the Third International Theory, and its most prominent characteristic was what he viewed as genuine democracy. In place of elected representatives was the rule of the masses—and a host of "people's" organizations.

Libya's plain green flag was adopted in 1977. Green is the national color of Libya. It is also a symbol of devotion to Islam. Many other Arab countries have incorporated green into their flags.

The official governing body of Libya is the General People's Congress (GPC). Consisting of more than 1,000 elected members (Libyans 18 and older have the franchise, and in fact voting is considered mandatory), the GPC meets several times a year.

Overseeing different areas of government (similar to the president's cabinet in the United States) is the General People's Committee, established by the GPC. Geographically, Libya is organized into military districts and municipal zones. These new zones do not coincide with longtime tribal boundaries. To the contrary, Qaddafi deliberately has broken up traditional tribal power centers, which he regards as potential threats to his system of government.

At local levels, a seemingly countless number of people's committees make decisions—at least in theory. Over time, Qaddafi authorized no fewer than 187 people's committees. This conformed with his philosophy that control should be in the hands of the people, not political parties or other centers of power. One practical problem with this arrangement is that under the Qaddafi regime, people's committee members have learned they might be blamed and punished if problems arise. Thus they have been afraid to make decisions.

Though Qaddafi and his followers claim that their country has no "government" at all, the Great Socialist People's Libyan Arab Jamahiriya is, on paper at least, a government administered by committees. But observers have noted the contradictions of Qaddafi's revolutionary government. Qaddafi sees Libya as a country in which the people have direct control over everything. "In reality," writes Dirk Vandewalle, editor of *Qadhafi's Libya, 1969–1994*, "Libya remains a political system where its leader and a few close advisors make virtually all decisions regarding economic and political development and deliberately exclude the most crucial economic sectors from direct popular management."

JUDICIAL SYSTEM

As mentioned previously, Qaddafi made *Sharia* the basis of Libya's legal system. This included traditional punishments prescribed by Islamic law—for example, that thieves have their hands cut off.

For practical purposes, a variety of courts (criminal, civil, commercial, military, and "people's courts") handle legal matters. Civil law is based on the Italian legal system.

Libya's highest court is its national Supreme Court. Headquartered in Tripoli, the Supreme Court has five separate court chambers, each of them presided over by five justices.

THE MILITARY

Military service is mandatory for both men and women. Active service in the army—by far the largest branch of the Libyan military—is for three years. Those in the air force and navy serve four-year terms. Libya's small navy performs basically a coast guard role, but it is bolstered by several Russian-made submarines. While he believed that Libya should ally itself neither with the Western nations (the United States was particularly hated for its support of Israel, the archenemy of the Arab world) nor the Soviet bloc, for pragmatic reasons Qaddafi turned to the USSR and East Germany for weapons and technical advisers during the 1970s and 1980s.

ECONOMIC OVERVIEW

Libya's abundant reserves of low-sulfur oil are crucial to the country's economy. Oil contributes nearly all of Libya's export earnings and accounts for about 25 percent of its **gross domestic product (GDP)**, the total value of goods and services the country produces annually. Libya's estimated GDP in 2008 stood at $89 billion (using the purchasing power parity method, which is designed to account for variations in the exchange rate of national currencies). GDP per capita—each Libyan's average share of the nation's economic activity—was estimated at $14,400. Libya has one of the highest per capita GDPs in Africa. So relatively speaking, it is a fairly prosperous country.

Yet the statistics fail to reflect several realities. First, there is considerable economic disparity across Libyan society, and petroleum revenues do not necessarily trickle down to benefit the poorest Libyans. In Libya's government-directed socialist economy, inefficient allocation of resources has contributed to chronic shortages of even basic goods and foodstuffs. In the early 1980s, for example, Qaddafi let committees of workers take over small businesses that had been operated privately, and he encouraged citizens to buy only from state-approved food stores. Mismanagement resulted in essential items falling into short supply, while factories made nonessential goods for which there was little demand. By the end of the decade, the government was forced to revive a form of privately run business.

Under the slogan "Partners, Not Wage Earners!" Qaddafi issued another strange decree: that privately owned businesses could employ only family members because the wage system exploits workers. Furthermore, he hinted that in Libya money might be abolished, to be replaced by the barter system (in which people

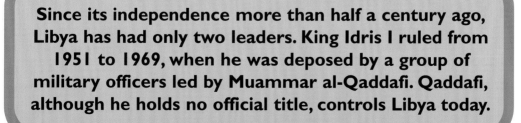

Since its independence more than half a century ago, Libya has had only two leaders. King Idris I ruled from 1951 to 1969, when he was deposed by a group of military officers led by Muammar al-Qaddafi. Qaddafi, although he holds no official title, controls Libya today.

trade goods and services directly). Not surprisingly, economic activity came to a near standstill, and this initiative, too, had to be abandoned. But by 2004 unemployment in Libya was estimated at 30 percent.

Given its oil reserves, Libya should be more prosperous. In addition to government mismanagement of the economy and Qaddafi's bizarre, shifting policies, United Nations–sponsored economic sanctions in effect between 1992 and 1999—imposed in response to Libyan sponsorship of international terrorism—hit hard.

AGRICULTURE

Libya's land and extremely dry climate are highly unsuitable for agriculture. More than 90 percent of the land is desert or semi-desert, and only 1 percent is arable (suitable for growing crops). An additional 8 percent can support some livestock grazing. Because of the harshness of the conditions, Libya must import three-quarters of its food, even though 17 percent of the Libyan people are involved in agriculture and the country has a small population to support.

As of old, farming activity is concentrated along the Mediterranean coast. Libya's chief crops are cereal grains: barley, wheat, and sorghum. Farmers also maintain fruit and almond orchards where the land permits. Italian colonists during the early 1900s developed olive plantations in the north, where olive production continues today.

Date palm trees are common in some cities and fertile areas and in the Saharan oases. Desert dwellers make use of the entire date palm tree. Besides eating the dates and using them in various types of food preparation, they weave the fronds into baskets, sandals, and other items. They use the wood for building materials and fuel.

Like their ancestors, many Libyans today earn their living by raising livestock, especially goats. They also raise cattle, sheep, camels, donkeys, and horses, grazing them in tribal lands. Some of the herd animals provide milk. They ultimately are slaughtered for their meat and hides; animal skins are among the limited products Libya has to export.

Camel owners take full advantage of a carcass when the animal dies. They make lard of the fat that forms its hump and various leather goods from its hide. While the animal is alive, they often dry its dung to burn for fuel.

Libyans still use camels for transportation, especially in the desert, although cars, trucks, and buses are common throughout the country. Farmers also engage these legendary beasts, as well as mules and horses, to pull ploughs.

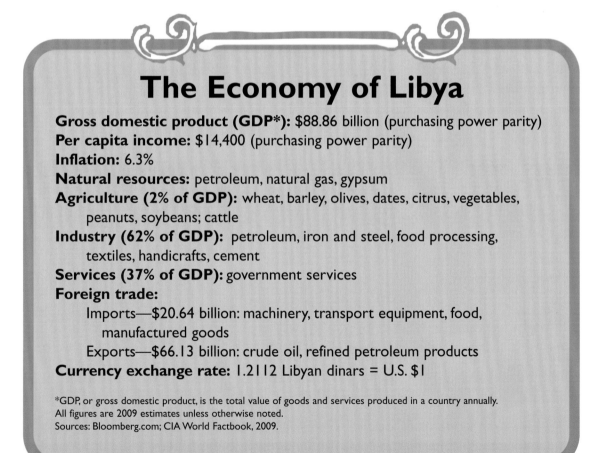

The Economy of Libya

Gross domestic product (GDP*): $88.86 billion (purchasing power parity)

Per capita income: $14,400 (purchasing power parity)

Inflation: 6.3%

Natural resources: petroleum, natural gas, gypsum

Agriculture (2% of GDP): wheat, barley, olives, dates, citrus, vegetables, peanuts, soybeans; cattle

Industry (62% of GDP): petroleum, iron and steel, food processing, textiles, handicrafts, cement

Services (37% of GDP): government services

Foreign trade:

Imports—$20.64 billion: machinery, transport equipment, food, manufactured goods

Exports—$66.13 billion: crude oil, refined petroleum products

Currency exchange rate: 1.2112 Libyan dinars = U.S. $1

*GDP, or gross domestic product, is the total value of goods and services produced in a country annually. All figures are 2009 estimates unless otherwise noted.
Sources: Bloomberg.com; CIA World Factbook, 2009.

A Libyan farmer uses a camel to plow his field. Only a very small area of Libya along the Mediterranean coast can be farmed, so the country must import most of its food.

The livestock trade in Libya is not without problems. Apart from the difficult climate, overgrazing of cattle and cultivation of the limited land have seriously taxed the soil along the edge of the Sahara.

In the late 20th century, the Libyan government began experimenting with projects to develop agriculture and control some of the desert dunes. For example, grass has been planted to prevent wind erosion in some areas. Liquid waste from oil refineries has been spread over the dunes to stabilize them. During the 1980s and 1990s, to bring water supplies into certain areas of the land, the government sponsored a pipeline system involving more than 1,000 miles (1,609 km) of construction. The main pipelines are enormous—at 13 feet (4 meters) in diameter, they are more than twice the height of the average human. The objective of this "Great Man-Made River," reportedly the world's most extensive water development project, is to transport water from natural reserves found beneath the Sahara to developing areas in the north, including Tripoli, Benghazi, Tobruk (also spelled Tubruq), and Surt. Some environmentalists have protested that the plan will lower water tables beneath the desert, eventually causing oasis wells to run dry.

THE PETROLEUM INDUSTRY

Libya's most important natural resource—and the basis of its entire economy—is oil. Most of Libya's petroleum reserves are located in the north, in the Surt Basin. Estimating the earth's oil reserves is a complicated, inexact undertaking, but it's believed that Libya has approximately 2 percent of the world's untapped petroleum. Crude oil from Libya is particularly desirable because it contains fairly low amounts of sulfur, which means that when burned in factories and automobiles it does not produce as much pollution as oil from other regions.

At the time of independence in 1951, Libya was one of the poorest countries in the world. Most Libyans were nomadic herders or subsistence farmers who grew just enough food for their families and villages to live on. There was no substantial industry. Libya's natural resources were so limited that one of the country's leading exports was scrap armor left abandoned in the desert by German and Allied armies during World War II.

Beginning in 1956, however, petroleum was discovered in separate locations in the two northern regions, Tripolitania and Cyrenaica. Oil revenues quickly transformed Libya. The government enthusiastically expanded programs; the country bustled with the building of pipelines, communication systems, and various construction projects. Qaddafi, to a greater extent than his predecessor, used oil income for social welfare programs. He doubled the minimum wage for workers and lowered the rent in government-owned apartments. He built up Libya's cities and improved its hospitals and schools. Libyans' standard of living improved markedly. By the 1970s, average incomes for Libyans were twice those of people in Italy, the region's former colonial master.

But the benefits of an economy based on the exporting of oil have not come without complications. For example, prices in the world oil market are prone to fluctuate. And as history has shown time and again, any country whose economy depends on a single export item will encounter trouble sooner or later. When the oil market declined during the late 1970s and early 1980s, Libya's economy suffered, and projects to develop other industries and farming had to be abandoned. By the late 1990s, despite its petroleum reserves, Libya's foreign debt had risen to more than $10 billion. Qaddafi warned that oil "is not a magic wand. It is a raw material, and its value is limited." Other difficulties have emerged from Libya's membership in the Organization of Petroleum Exporting Countries (OPEC), a group of 11 major oil-producing nations in Africa, Asia, and South America. OPEC regulates crude oil prices among its member nations, and Qaddafi has frequently

The head of Libya's National Oil Corporation Shukri Ghanem talks to reporters following the announcement of gas-prospecting licenses in Tripoli, December 2007. As part of opening the country up to foreign investment, Libya awarded gas exploration contracts to outside companies.

been at odds with the organization's policies. In fact, the Libyan leader has at times thumbed his nose at OPEC and arranged petroleum transactions in violation of the organization's decisions.

OTHER INDUSTRY

Apart from its oil works, Libya is not a highly developed industrial country. Many of its industries are petroleum-related. For example, Libyan companies make pipeline parts and oil storage containers.

Libya also is an important producer of natural gas. The largest gas liquefaction plant in the world is at Marsa al-Burayqah. Other small factories—some with fewer than 100 employees—process foods, including salt, and produce such goods as cement, cloth, and leather items.

Although Libya is a coastal country, fishing is not a major part of its economy. Libya's catch includes sardines, tuna, and mullet from the Mediterranean Sea. Fishing fleets from other Mediterranean nations buy permits from Libya's government. Libyan waters are noted especially for their rich sponge beds.

Libya has a merchant marine fleet of only about 30 cargo, tanker, and short-route passenger ships. With such a limited number of ships, it has to export most of its oil in the tankers of other nations.

LABOR SHORTAGES

Libya's relatively sparse population was never able to supply enough skilled workers for Qaddafi's ambitious development projects. Libya has had to bring in foreign workers, mostly from neighboring countries. At one time, Libya was employing almost a million foreign workers, many of them industrial and military technical experts who commanded top salaries. In the early 1980s, it was estimated that more than half of Libya's teachers were Egyptian

An artisan works in the old city, or medina, of Tripoli.

nationals. By and large, higher-paying jobs were held by Egyptians, Palestinians, Moroccans, and Tunisians, as well as Eastern Europeans and Koreans. Migrant workers from Chad and Sudan performed much of the unskilled labor.

This foreign labor proved unduly expensive in Libya's economy. But when the government cut back on the number of internationals working in the country, development efforts stalled.

RELIGION

Libya is officially an Islamic nation. And an overwhelming percentage of the Libyan people practice the Muslim faith.

The beginnings of the Islamic religion date to around A.D. 610, when the prophet Muhammad, an Arab merchant living in Mecca, a town in present-day Saudi Arabia, claimed to have been visited by an angel of Allah (God). Muhammad began to preach God's revealed message, first secretly to family members, friends, and a few others, then publicly. The core of his message—that there is only one true God—did not sit well among the idol-worshipping, polytheistic Meccans. Eventually, in 622, persecution forced Muhammad and his followers—called Muslims—to flee to the oasis town of Medina. That event, known as the Hegira, or Hijra, marks the beginning of the Islamic era. After several years of warfare, Muhammad and his followers captured Mecca, in 629. By the time of his death three years later, the entire Arabian Peninsula had come under the influence of Islam. In the following decades, Muslims would spread their religion—and build a large empire—through conquest.

Muslims believe that there is only one God, that Muhammad is his last and most important prophet, and that God's words are contained in the Qur'an (also spelled Koran), a collection of revelations received by Muhammad.

The vast majority of Libyans—some 97 percent—belong to the Sunni branch of the Muslim faith, which is also the dominant

The Qur'an, the holy book of Islam. Fully 97 percent of Libyans are Muslim. The majority follow Sunni Islam, the most common form of the faith. Islamic law, or Sharia, is the basis of Libya's legal system.

branch of Islam worldwide; only a very small minority of Libyans are Shiites. The two groups originally split in the seventh century over the issue of how to choose **caliphs**, Muhammad's successors as leaders of the *umma*, the Islamic "community of believers." Sunnis hold that caliphs can be elected and count Abu Bakr, a devout disciple of the Prophet, as the first caliph. Shiites believe a caliph must be a direct descendant of Muhammad; they view Ali, the Prophet's son-in-law, as the first legitimate caliph, though he was historically Islam's fourth leader after Muhammad's death.

In Libya, not only is Islam the state religion, but the Qur'an is regarded as the nation's ultimate law book, the code by which Libyans must live. The official government policy is that all other laws are secondary to the teachings of the Qur'an.

Shortly after he came to power, Qaddafi told a journalist that the Qur'an contains "the answers to all your questions." He outlawed Christianity and made Islam central to all aspects of Libyan life. His zealotry for Islam has inspired him to promote it as the national religion of other African countries, not just his own.

Yet it would be incorrect to suggest that conservative **Islamists**—who also seek to establish Islamic governments and societies in other nations—support Libya's leader. Qaddafi's liberal policies have often put him at odds with Muslim fundamentalists. While the Qur'an teaches that men are superior to women, under Qaddafi's rule women have gained more liberties and opportunities. Writing in the December 2000 issue of *National Geographic*, journalist Andrew Cockburn observed that before Qaddafi's cultural revolution, women when appearing in public "were almost invariably invisible behind the all-encompassing traditional white *furushiya* [veil], and the number of female university graduates numbered just 35. Today, the *furushiya* has all but disappeared, and the number of women graduating from universities exceeds that of men." Plus, in Qaddafi's Libya, women serve in the military.

A family visits the beach at Tripoli. Today about 78 percent of Libyans live in urban areas.

The People

Fully 97 percent of Libya's people claim ancestry from either the Berbers—various nomadic peoples who inhabited North Africa as early as 3000 B.C.—or from the Arabs who conquered the region in the seventh century A.D. Over the centuries, most of Libya's Berbers have become thoroughly Arabized. The few who continue to cling to their ancestors' customs and language live in small villages in western Libya or, in the case of the Tuareg people, are nomads in the desert southwest. Berbers generally are light-skinned, tall, and strong. Their women live in concealment, and Berber clans take pride in their independence. Most Berbers live in western Libya.

Among the minority groups in modern-day Libya are ethnic Europeans and Asians, as well as Africans from the interior of the continent. Many in the latter group—particularly in the Fezzan and Tripolitania regions—are black-skinned descendants of slaves who were brought north in previous centuries via the torturous Sahara caravan routes. Once in Libya these slaves were forced to work as domestic servants or soldiers. Eventually they became integrated into Libyan society, and today many of their descendants have moved to cities, where they typically work in unskilled, low-paying jobs. Many of those in rural areas farm for a living.

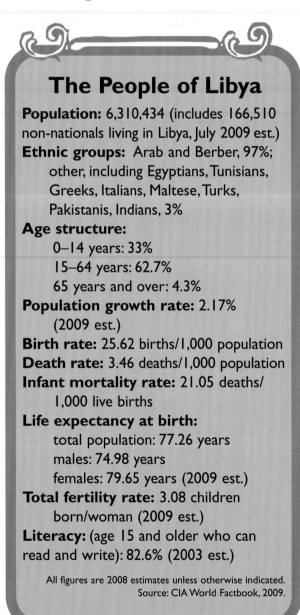

The People of Libya

Population: 6,310,434 (includes 166,510 non-nationals living in Libya, July 2009 est.)

Ethnic groups: Arab and Berber, 97%; other, including Egyptians, Tunisians, Greeks, Italians, Maltese, Turks, Pakistanis, Indians, 3%

Age structure:
  0–14 years: 33%
  15–64 years: 62.7%
  65 years and over: 4.3%

Population growth rate: 2.17% (2009 est.)

Birth rate: 25.62 births/1,000 population

Death rate: 3.46 deaths/1,000 population

Infant mortality rate: 21.05 deaths/1,000 live births

Life expectancy at birth:
  total population: 77.26 years
  males: 74.98 years
  females: 79.65 years (2009 est.)

Total fertility rate: 3.08 children born/woman (2009 est.)

Literacy: (age 15 and older who can read and write): 82.6% (2003 est.)

All figures are 2008 estimates unless otherwise indicated.
Source: CIA World Factbook, 2009.

During the Qaddafi era, foreign access to the country has been tightly controlled. Rarely has the Libyan government granted travel visas to foreigners except for employment purposes. And men serving in the Libyan government are permitted to marry only Arab women. This is in keeping with Qaddafi's vision of Libya as an Arab nation "unpolluted" by foreign ideas and practices.

TRIBAL CONNECTIONS

From early times, nomadic peoples have roamed the deserts of North Africa with their camels, goats, and sheep, constantly seeking grazing areas and water holes. A water hole that supplied them on one visit might have run dry when they returned in a year or two. They took advantage of the rare oases that dotted the desert,

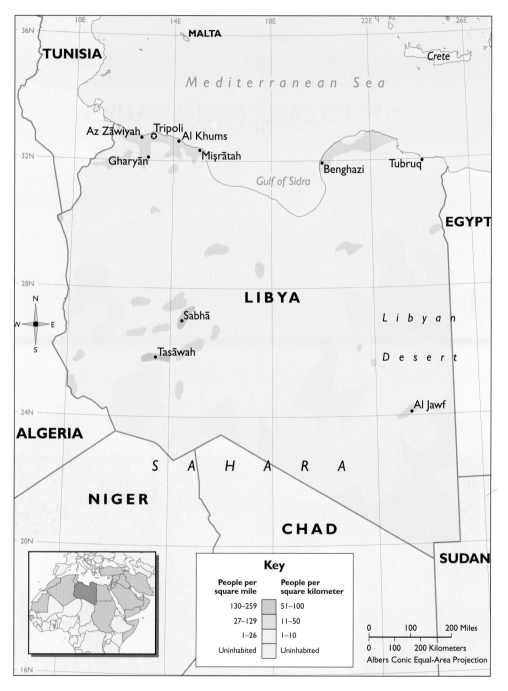

Libya is sparsely populated, as this map indicates. Overall, the country has a population density of just about 8 people per square mile (3 people per square kilometer). However, this is a misleading figure, as most of the country's 6.3 million people live near the Mediterranean coast.

but the first Libyans did not establish villages or towns around them. They lived in tents, giving them the freedom to relocate at will. Their scant population was—and to some extent still is—organized around families and tribes. It's estimated that at one time, almost 90 percent of the people dwelling in what is now Libya belonged to tribal groups.

Tribes still live in the deserts of Libya, most of them in oasis settlements. Oasis farmers can still be observed drawing well water with rope pulleys and goatskin bags. Certain Berber people make their homes in hillside caves around Gharyan, some 50 miles (80 km) south of Tripoli. While this lifestyle may sound primitive, their cave dwellings are surprisingly sophisticated and comfortable—relatively cool in the summer heat and warm in the winter chill.

Libyan life changed markedly in the second half of the 20th

A farmer carries a newborn camel at his farm in the village of Qasr al-Ghashir.

century. When Libya became independent in 1951, only 16 percent of its people lived in towns and cities. Since then, the trend has been reversed. An estimated two-thirds of Libyans now live in Tripolitania near the northwestern coast. In all, about 78 percent of Libyans live in urban areas. Nomads and village people moved to the cities in search of jobs and better living conditions.

At the same time, the government in many ways has modernized remote villages, supplying electricity, water systems, telephones, hospitals, schools, and TV and radio. Sabhah, an oasis deep in the heart of the western desert, was irrigated to nurture farming; the town even became the site of a large airport.

Despite the changes brought about by modernization, most Libyans still are influenced by the **qabilah**, or tribe, to which they belong. The basic unit of Libyan social structure is the family. A group of extended families forms a clan, or **lahma**. A group of clans forms a tribe. On holidays, many Libyans proudly dress in the tradition of their ancestors, while performers render songs and dances handed down through many generations.

THE BEDOUINS

Arabic-speaking Muslims, the Bedouin people are desert dwellers whose traditional lifestyle involves moving their camels, sheep, goats, and other livestock across the barren land in a constant search for grazing areas and drinking water. The Bedouins live in tents and rely on their animals to provide many of their necessities. They make clothes of hides and eat dairy products derived from the milk of their herds. For other essentials—tools, knives, cooking utensils, and various food items—they trade the hides, meat, and milk produced by their livestock with people of the villages and towns they encounter.

The Bedouins, a proud and fiercely independent group, have always lived by a remarkable code of honor. They are generous to strangers and consider it their responsibility to provide water and food to those in dire need—even mortal enemies. They have been known to steal cattle, but not living necessities such as tents. Their first loyalty is to their tribe, and an insult to a family's honor may spark a violent intertribal feud with long-lasting effects.

The wandering Bedouin lifestyle seriously waned in the late 20th century. The Bedouins cannot avoid entirely the effects of modernization. Many of the village families with whom they once traded have moved to larger towns and cities, attracted by jobs, health care, education, and other benefits. Some of the Bedouins themselves have abandoned the nomadic life.

THE TUAREG

Another close-knit minority are the Tuareg nomads of southwestern Libya. The Tuareg inhabit portions of the Sahara Desert and, further southward, steppe and savanna country, stretching across national boundaries, from Algeria and Libya to Mauritania, Senegal, Nigeria, Niger, Mali, Burkina Faso, and Chad. In ancient times, Tuareg people did not farm or herd but made their living by raiding caravans and settlements of other desert peoples. They carried away slaves and demanded tribute from caravanners in return for unmolested passage. Predictably, as the era of the caravans and the slave trade passed, they were cast into poverty.

The Tuareg are unique in that over the centuries, women in significant ways became more prominent than men within their culture. For example, women became the property holders and heirs. They read and write, and they carry on Tuareg musical traditions, performing on the lute and other instruments. The Tuareg are notable in appearance for their full dress—approximately 10 feet of cloth wrapping—with only their eyes exposed, lending an air of intrigue.

The Tuareg of southwestern Libya are nomadic desert people known for their traditional blue clothing. Most members of this minority group make their living by raising livestock, trading, and farming.

WOMEN, MEN, AND THE FAMILY

Libyan women, although quite liberated in comparison with women in other Muslim nations, still live largely "protected"—and somewhat subservient—lives. Libyan women serve in the military and attend universities, but they are expected to perform largely domestic duties: housekeeping and child rearing. Within the family, the father is the undisputed decision maker, and in some homes women have their own rooms where men are forbidden. Among communities who observe strict, traditional Arab customs, women are expected to follow the Muslim custom of keeping their faces veiled. Even women who don't veil their faces are expected to dress modestly, avoiding short skirts and other fashions designed to reveal bare flesh.

Muslim men may have several wives, although most Libyan men have just one. A man must have his first wife's permission in order to marry a second, and Islam requires that the husband treat all his wives equally. A woman may have only one husband.

Under Islamic teaching, a man can divorce his wife with no stated reason. In modern Libya, women likewise have been given divorce rights. When a couple divorces, their daughters typically live with the mother, their sons with the father.

Among desert peoples, men are expected to marry and produce many offspring. The number of children a man has both reflects and influences the tribal standing of his family. The custom of having numerous children is an old one, common to many cultures on different continents, especially among rural peoples. Before the industrial era, sons and daughters were needed to help work farmland, earn a living for the family, and provide for their parents in their old age.

In most cases, marriages in Libya are arranged. If a young couple wants to become engaged on their own initiative, they must win the approval not just of their parents but also of cousins, uncles, and aunts.

Until recent times, Libyan girls were not sent to school, since homemaking was to be their vocation. Many Libyan women today obtain higher education for professional careers, typically as teachers, nurses, and clerical workers. But the idea of a woman going into the city to work for a living is appalling to Muslims who follow traditional teachings. This is the kind of issue that causes considerable tension in Libya today between modern and fundamentalist Muslims.

Libyans today, like their ancestors, and like Arab society in general, maintain strong family units with strict rules. Older people are treated with special respect because of their wisdom and their status in the family. When a person grows old, he or she almost always receives care from the younger family members at home, not nurses and aides at a home for the aged.

Youngsters are expected to be obedient. Children are brought up to contribute to the household, performing chores around the home as soon as they are old enough to make themselves useful. When they join scouting programs, they enjoy camping and recreational activities much like other scouts worldwide, but in Libya the emphasis is on community service projects.

Most Libyans are carefully courteous to everyone they meet in public. Criticism, by custom, is expressed only in private. Muslims frequently mention the name of Allah in ordinary conversation—phrases such as "Allah is good" and "Praise Allah" are frequently heard, for example. Although they are respectful of strangers, they typically invite only friends and relatives inside their homes.

CLOTHING

In times past, typical Libyan clothing consisted of long, flowing robes and scarves or turbans. Today, Libyans who live in the desert still dress this way. Although long robes might look uncomfortably hot to the unknowing observer, they actually are light and keep the body cool from the relentless sun.

But Western clothing styles also have been adopted, especially in the cities. People commonly wear jeans and open-necked shirts, or European-style fashions. Professional workers often wear business suits. Some people clothe themselves in a combination of traditional and Western attire. For example, a woman might appear in a modern skirt and blouse, but with a scarf on her head. Men sometimes wear the familiar fez, a brimless red hat common to northern Africa. Libyan women like to wear jewelry, particularly on special occasions.

HEALTH AND MEDICAL CARE

The Qaddafi government has encouraged large families, and despite an infant death rate that is more than three times higher than the rate in the United States, Libya's population is growing at a comparatively high rate (an estimated 2.2 percent in 2009, compared

In Islamic literature it is written, "Allah is beautiful and He loves beauty." Thus, ornamentation is an important aspect of many buildings in Libya and throughout the Muslim world. Intricate tilework, particularly geometric patterns such as the one shown here, is common.

with 0.98 percent for the United States). The country has a young average population: a third of its people are 15 or younger.

The Qaddafi regime has made Libya a welfare state, using oil income to fund free medical care for the people. In the first 15 years of Qaddafi's rule, the number of doctors and dentists in Libya reportedly rose to seven times the number available during the reign of King Idris. (Some medical students are educated in Libya, but most study abroad.) During the same period, the number of hospital beds tripled. Major hospitals are at Tripoli and Benghazi, with dozens of smaller hospitals and clinics scattered around the country. The state also funds workers' medical benefits and retirement pensions.

Modern Libya has made progress in reducing traditional health threats. Malaria, once a dreaded disease among Libyans, has been conquered, and the incidence of other serious maladies, such as leprosy and tuberculosis, has diminished. However, typhoid, rabies, intestinal disorders (usually resulting from poor drinking water), and other serious diseases continue to pose problems.

EDUCATION

Libya has a higher literacy rate than most African and some Arab countries: more than 80 percent of Libyans age 15 and older can read and write. Six years of primary schooling is required for all Libyan children. Some continue their education with three years of intermediate study, during which they may begin to learn a vocation, followed by three more years of advanced learning. State-sponsored institutions of higher learning are Al-Fateh University in Tripoli and Garyounis University in Benghazi. Some Libyans are able to study in foreign countries—Arab as well as Western. The government also has encouraged adult education.

THE ARTS, LITERATURE, AND THE MEDIA

The arts in Libya have government support, but they must conform to Muslim doctrine. Paintings and drawings are abstract or geometric rather than realistic. That's because Islam teaches that if an artist creates a natural portrayal of a person or animal, the subject loses part of his or her soul. For the same reason, Muslim leaders frown on photography as an art form.

Artistic skills are displayed not only in paintings but also in windows and on walls. Potters and other craft workers produce impressive items. The city of Misratah is famous for its carpets. Muslims carry specially designed prayer rugs on which to kneel

Arabic is Libya's official language and is spoken by practically all Libyans. Although the Libyan government under Muammar Qaddafi was unfriendly for many years toward the United States and other capitalist Western countries, the English language is common among Libyans who have international business dealings.

and pray at the appointed times of day. In addition to geometric shapes, flower designs are popular.

Qaddafi's regime has encouraged the preservation of age-old folk skills and customs. These include traditional dances as well as folk crafts—weaving, wood-carving, metalworking, and embroidery, among others.

Arabic is Libya's official language. As in all Arabic-speaking countries, the classical Arabic of the Qur'an coexists with Modern Standard Arabic, used in education and the media, and more popular forms of the language used in everyday speech. In several remote places, Berbers still speak variations of Tamazight, the language of their ancestors.

Until the late 20th century, religious writings based on the Qur'an were the only form of literature available to most Libyans. When Qaddafi came to power, he began to allow writers and poets a degree of free expression. The government boasts that it allows a free press, but this is true only insofar as what the press says conforms with the teachings of *The Green Book* and the Qur'an. Since the government tightly controls book, newspaper, and magazine distribution in the country, it is difficult for authors with different points of view to get their writings into print. Foreign periodicals and books are forbidden. Foreign journalists who have been critical of the Qaddafi government are refused admission to the country.

The government also oversees Libya's broadcast media. Television and radio broadcasts are in Arabic, with limited English,

Italian, and French translations in some areas. Teachings from *The Green Book* frequently are broadcast; one national television channel focuses entirely on educating viewers concerning Qaddafi's policies.

Libya has a limited number of movie theaters. They show foreign films (with Arabic subtitles or overdubs), but the movies are closely censored.

Libyan museums contain artifacts from the long history not just of Libya but of North Africa generally. They are exceptionally important to archaeologists and others who study natural sciences and history. Among the most prominent is the Tripoli Museum of Archaeology and Prehistory.

Architecture in Libya illustrates the many influences the country has experienced over the centuries. The largest cities feature buildings of majestic Saharan design as well as modern high-rise apartment complexes not unlike those in America.

An aerial view of Tripoli, the largest city and capital of Libya. Located on the Mediterranean Sea, Tripoli has a metropolitan-area population of about 1.7 million people.

Communities

Libya's most important cities are located in the north, along the Mediterranean coast. As the country's population becomes more urban, these cities will continue to grow.

TRIPOLI

Tripoli, a historic city on the northwestern coast, is Libya's capital and major seaport. With a population of about 1.7 million, the Tripoli metropolitan area is home to approximately one-quarter of the country's people.

A bustling, growing city, Tripoli is noted as a comparatively clean metropolis among the world's capitals. It is a place of marked historical contrast. Looking out over the beautiful Mediterranean are battlements preserved from centuries past. Heavy guns here once protected Tripoli from naval attack. In the Roman quarter, or the "Old City," the marble arched entryway dates to the second century A.D. As

Tourists wander from ancient ruins to beaches at Leptis Magna. The Phoenicians established the city as a trading post in the sixth century B.C.; it later became an important Roman city in North Africa.

in days of old, merchants in myriad stalls, or **souks**, sell manufactured products, crafts, jewelry, and fresh food.

With the old resides the new. Tripoli is a city under construction, a metropolis of modern high-rise apartments and university pods. Bumper-to-bumper traffic regularly clogs certain parts of the city, while donkey carts occasionally can be seen clip-clopping along the edges of Tripoli's paved streets. The docks are alive with the activities of an international shipping industry. **Mosques**, both new and old, are found throughout the city and are used not just as centers of prayer but as meeting halls.

BENGHAZI

Libya's other major city, Benghazi, is also a Mediterranean port. Situated in the Cyrenaica region in the northeast, where the coastline dips southward to form the Gulf of Sidra, Benghazi has approximately half as many residents as Tripoli. Like the Libyan capital, Benghazi combines the modern and the ancient in its architecture. However, its people tend toward more traditional dress and customs than do residents of Tripoli.

The oil boom of the 1960s fueled significant growth in Benghazi. Petroleum extracted from major oil fields nearby was pumped directly to Benghazi for export, making the city a vital oil port.

OTHER CITIES

After Tripoli and Benghazi, Libya's most important ports are Tobruk and Misratah. Situated at the western edge of the Gulf of Sidra, Misratah is the third-largest city in Libya. It is noted for its colorful carpet markets. Tobruk, on the northwestern coast near the Egyptian border, has a major oil refinery, processing crude oil from deep within Cyrenaica. During World War II, Tobruk was the site of an epic tank battle between German and British forces.

Darnah, Marsa al-Burayqah, Al Khums, and Zuwarah are among Libya's other important ports.

URBAN LIFE

Life in cities like Tripoli and Benghazi is very different from life in rural areas. Besides being seaports, Tripoli and Benghazi are university cities. Thus residents are more likely to be exposed to ideas and influences from abroad—even though the government has taken pains to limit its citizens' access to information. Residents in Libya's cities generally enjoy a decent standard of living thanks to the country's petroleum income. They also tend to be relatively well educated.

Many inhabitants of the cities live in modern high-rise apartments. Professional workers, military officers, government officials, and foreign experts employed by the government reside in attractive homes, many of them with central courtyards and flowered patios, and they enjoy a comfortable lifestyle. Libyan cities are not without slum communities, though. The poor live in small apartments, some with inadequate lighting and sanitation, or in shanties surrounding the cities.

In the interior towns, residents live in mud-brick houses. These homes usually have flat roofs and tiny windows.

TRANSPORTATION

Libya has more than 62,100 miles (almost 100,000 km) of roads, mostly unpaved. The major highway runs east-west along the coast between the Egyptian and Tunisian borders; it is more than 1,000 miles (1,609 km) long. Other roads, both paved and unpaved, connect Tripoli and other major northern cities to remote towns in the central and southern regions. Libya manufactures no trucks or automobiles, so all vehicles must be imported. Qaddafi has banned the importation of American-made autos.

Limited rail lines were established in North Africa during the colonial period, but Libya has had no railroads in operation since the mid-1960s.

International airports serve Tripoli, Benghazi, and Sabhah, while about 130 airfields accommodate local flights. Fewer than half the airports have (or require) paved runways. Libyan Arab Airlines is the national airline.

HOLIDAYS AND OBSERVANCES

Libyans follow the Islamic lunar calendar, by which a year is about 354 days long, rather than the 365-day Western, or

Gregorian, calendar. In the Islamic calendar, each month begins when the crescent moon first becomes visible to a human observer after a new moon.

For Libyans, as for Muslims throughout the world, A.D. 622—the year of Muhammad's flight from Mecca, or Hijra (Hegira)—constitutes the beginning of year one of the Islamic era. Hijra Day—the Islamic New Year's Day—fell on January 10 and December 29 in 2008 (the years 1429 and 1430 in the Islamic calendar). Each year Muslims celebrate this day by remembering the life of Muhammad and by maintaining a spirit of well-wishing.

Each year during the holy month of Ramadan, Muslims fast during the daylight hours. In Libya, even non-Muslims are required to publicly obey the Ramadan fast. But Ramadan is also a time of celebration. At nightfall, Muslims eat a festive meal, with music and laughter. Fireworks and parades are part of the Ramadan observance as well. Ramadan ends with a festival called Eid al-Fitr, during which Muslims traditionally don new clothes to symbolize a new beginning in their lives. They also decorate their homes and exchange gifts.

A mosque in Tripoli. Because Islam is the predominant religion of Libya, Muslim rituals are an important part of everyday life.

At least once in their lifetime, Muslims who are able are expected to travel to the holy city of Mecca during the month of Dhu'l-Hijja. This pilgrimage is called the *hajj*. Some two million Muslims from around the world each year make the hajj. They spend approximately two weeks in Mecca, observing a series of rituals that climaxes in the Feast of Sacrifice (Eid al-Adha), which lasts several days. When they return home, pilgrims are greeted in celebration by their neighbors.

Other Islamic holy days include Lailat al-Barth and Tenth Muharram. Lailat al-Barth, or "Night of Forgiveness," occurs on the night of the full moon two weeks before the holy month of Ramadan; Muslims are supposed to forgive one another as part of their preparation for Ramadan. A solemn day of fasting among Muslims, Tenth Muharram commemorates the exodus of the Israelites from bondage in Egypt during the time of Moses, an epic event mentioned in both the Qur'an and the Bible's Old Testament.

Some mosques in Libya are simple gathering halls for worship. Others are impressive structures with colorful, lavish interior decoration. In the cities, a mosque official called the *muezzin* climbs to the top of the *minaret*, or mosque tower, and chantingly issues the call to prayer (either by loudspeaker or in a loud cry) five times each day. For Muslims prayer is required at dawn, noon, mid-afternoon, sunset, and before going to bed. Men and boys often go to the mosque to pray while women and girls pray at home. The whole family sometimes prays at home, placing their prayer mats on the floor.

Muslims may pray anywhere, anytime. In addition to regular formal prayers, Muslims offer private prayers to Allah as they feel the need. When they pray, Libyans face southeast toward Mecca, the birthplace of Muhammad. Sometimes they lean forward from their knees to touch their foreheads to the ground. Men pray with their palms opened upward. Women pray with their hands cupped.

Before praying inside a mosque, Muslims must ritually wash their faces and hands at the fountain outside.

The major prayer each week is the one at noon on Friday, the Muslim holy day (much like Saturday to Jews and Sunday to Christians). In mosques at this time, the local Islamic prayer leader, known as the **imam**, delivers a sermon. Businesses close on Fridays. After the midday prayer, Libyans relax and rest.

Besides religious observances, Libyans have a number of special national holidays. September 1, observed as National Day or Revolution Day, marks the anniversary of the night in 1969 when Qaddafi and the Free Unionist Officers seized power. Each year the event is celebrated with parades, military displays, and public speeches. It is Libya's equivalent to America's Fourth of July holiday.

Another political holiday is Independence Day, December 24, commemorating Libya's formal independence in 1951. Lesser holidays include Constitution Day (October 7) and Proclamation Day (November 21). A uniquely anti-American holiday is observed on June 11. Called Evacuation Day, it marks the withdrawal of U.S. troops from Wheelus Air Base in Libya; Wheelus was an important U.S. military post in the Mediterranean during the reign of King Idris.

MARRIAGE, DOMESTIC LIFE, AND FOOD

Weddings are both colorful and solemn occasions. In Libya the institution of marriage is taken quite seriously: the law calls for whipping an unmarried couple if the woman becomes pregnant. Wedding ceremonies are held at the home of the bride or at a mosque, followed by up to six days of traditional celebrations. In some weddings, the bride wears a dress with intricate, elaborate designs. The community's imam officiates. The marriage becomes official with the signing of a contract between the man and woman.

Families who live in apartments take their meals together.

In a photo taken around the time of Libya's independence, members of a band play traditional instruments on a street in Misratah.

Elsewhere, a traditional custom is that when a special meal is prepared, the men and women of the family eat separately—the men first. The family prays before and after eating. The oldest member of the family begins eating first unless a guest is present, in which case everyone courteously waits for the guest to start. Among the Bedouins, diners use no knives or forks but eat with their hands. Along the coast, families often go on holiday picnics to the beach.

The influences on Libyan cooking are both Mediterranean and Arabic. From the Italians, Libyans developed a strong preference for pasta. Bread is another staple of the Libyan diet. Libyans like to use a variety of spices in food preparation, and they also like sweets. Among those who can afford meat, lamb is most common, and chicken is also popular. Before slaughtering animals, butchers say a prayer as prescribed by Islamic teaching. Fresh vegetables and fruits, including olives, dates, figs, and apricots—are available along the coast. Beverages include mint tea, fruit juice, thick coffee, bottled cola, and spicy hot drinks.

Typically, breakfast for a Libyan family is a simple meal consisting of tea and bread, and perhaps **couscous** sweetened with honey. Couscous is one of the most common food preparations in this part of the world. In Libya, it is made with wheat flour, kneaded into balls with water and salt. Sometimes it is eaten plain, sometimes—in mid-afternoon meals or holiday feasts, for example—with vegetables.

Libyans are in the custom of taking a mid-afternoon meal—the biggest meal of the day—followed by a rest time. The weekday in Libya is divided into two parts. Business offices open at 7:00 or 8:00 A.M., close at 1:00 or 2:00 in the afternoon for the meal and rest break, and reopen from 4:00 to 6:30 P.M. Shops are open as late as 8:30 P.M.

One thing not commonly found in Libya, even at festive celebrations, is alcohol, which the government officially bans (Islam forbids believers to consume alcoholic beverages). Likewise, the eating of pork—considered unclean by Muslims—is forbidden in Libya.

ENTERTAINMENT

In Libya folk dances are common at festivals, as are horse races. Horse racing is extremely popular and in some respects is even considered a form of art. Horses are known to have been used in the region for more than 3,000 years. In fact, the chariot races made famous by the ancient Greeks and Romans were inspired by similar events they had witnessed in Libya. Libyans also race camels.

As in many other Middle Eastern and African countries, the most popular sport in Libya is soccer. Children play pickup games. Local soccer clubs are active, and Libyan teams compete internationally in Arab and African tournaments. However, worldwide competition for Libyan athletes has been limited during the Qaddafi era, and as of 2008 no Libyan had ever won an Olympic medal. Qaddafi has banned sports he considers brutal, including boxing and bullfighting.

Muammar al-Qaddafi speaks for the first time before the United Nations in his role as chair of the African Union, in February 2009. Since the late 1990s, the Libyan leader has worked to remake his image and increase Libya's stature internationally.

Foreign Relations

O ver four decades as Libya's leader, Muammar al-Qaddafi has authored a foreign policy characterized by fierce independence, belligerence, a degree of risk taking bordering on recklessness, and unpredictability. He has both sought Arab unity and battled Arab neighbors; fomented revolution in Africa, Asia, and South America; sponsored coup attempts and international terrorism; and incurred the wrath of the United States. Just as his domestic policies have largely insulated the Libyan people from outside influences, Qaddafi's foreign policy has frequently isolated his country, even within the Arab world. It was not until the late 1990s that Libya's leader began to adopt a more moderate foreign policy, and that approach has led to the country's improved relations with the international community.

UNFULFILLED DREAMS OF PAN-ARABISM

Insofar as his foreign policy can be said to display a consistent, coherent goal, Qaddafi's main ambition, regionally at least, has been to create a stronger and more united Arab world—under his leadership. Early on, he proposed a merger of Libya with Egypt, the neighboring land of his hero, Gamal Abdel Nasser. In 1972 Qaddafi and the leaders of Syria and Egypt actually formed a short-lived union of the three countries: the Federation of Arab Republics. A key objective of these initiatives, in Qaddafi's mind, was to mount a powerful, united force to oppose Israel. Egypt, he envisioned, would provide a sizeable military force; sparsely populated Libya could pump millions of dollars of oil revenues into the cause. But the Federation of Arab Republics soon dissolved.

Despite the failure of that and later efforts at unification (other proposed unions included Sudan, Malta, Tunisia, Chad, and Morocco), Qaddafi has relentlessly continued to preach his pan-Arab message. In the process, he has criticized Arab countries for what he regards as their overreliance on outside economic ties and their willingness to permit foreign corporations to gain a foothold in Arab affairs. (Shortly after he came to power, Qaddafi nationalized foreign-owned petroleum operations in Libya.) He has railed against what he calls "economic colonialism."

REGIONAL CONFLICTS

Such criticism is only one reason that leaders of other Arab nations regard Qaddafi warily. Over the course of his many years in power, the colonel has shown little hesitation about meddling in the affairs of neighbors, both Arab and non-Arab, through sponsorship of guerrilla organizations or terrorism or through direct military action. Qaddafi's armed forces have fought directly with Egypt, Chad, and Tunisia. In addition, Libya has supported guerrillas

A meeting of the Arab League, an organization that promotes the interests of Arab states. Libya has been a member since 1953. Qaddafi has been a frequent critic of the League, because of frustration with its response to the Israeli-Palestinian conflict and other Middle Eastern issues. Libya threatened to withdraw from the organization in October 2002, but retracted that announcement the following January.

fighting Morocco over control of the disputed Western Sahara region (on Africa's northwestern coast), as well as Lebanese militias (at the eastern end of the Mediterranean), not to mention revolutionary groups as far afield as South Africa, Colombia, the Philippines, Japan, and Ireland.

In 1980 Qaddafi backed a revolt in Tunisia, Libya's neighbor to the northwest. The incident worsened already-strained relations between the two countries—a situation dating to 1974 when Tunisian president Habib Bourguiba rejected Qaddafi's overtures of unification. Tunisia and Libya also were at odds over ownership of certain offshore oil reserves.

Similar tensions prevailed with Libya's neighbor to the southeast, Sudan. Jaafar an Numayri, Sudan's president, claimed that Qaddafi was behind a succession of plots to overthrow his regime during the 1970s. Numayri was also troubled by Libya's interference in the affairs of Sudan's western neighbor, Chad. In 1981 the Sudanese president called on the Arab League to cut its ties with Libya and to advocate the ouster of Qaddafi from power—by force, if necessary. Soon afterward, Chad's embassy in Sudan was bombed; Libyan involvement was suspected.

Libya's relations with the government of Chad had grown increasingly hostile. Since the mid-1960s a civil war had been raging in Chad, and in 1971 Qaddafi began supplying the rebel forces in that conflict. Though the rebels were fellow Muslims, Qaddafi's motivations weren't entirely religious; he coveted a region in the Tibesti Mountains of northern Chad that was believed to contain rich mineral deposits, including uranium—which can be used in nuclear weapons. In 1973 Libyan troops invaded Chad and occupied a parcel of territory along the northern border known as the Aozou Strip.

In the early 1980s the new government of Chad requested that Libyan troops withdraw. Libya refused, and Qaddafi renewed claims that the Aozou Strip was properly Libyan territory. Open fighting broke out between Libyan and Chadian forces in 1987, with France and the United States aiding the latter. Ultimately, the Chadian forces defeated Qaddafi's army, driving the Libyans out and capturing millions of dollars worth of abandoned military armament. Although the two nations agreed to a truce and renewed their severed diplomatic ties, Qaddafi's regime was suspected of involvement in a 1990 coup attempt against the Chadian government. In 1994 the International Court of Justice ruled that the Aozou Strip belonged to Chad, a decision Qaddafi accepted.

TROUBLED RELATIONS WITH EGYPT

After a brief prospect for union with Egypt in the early 1970s, Libyan-Egyptian relations deteriorated dramatically. Qaddafi branded Anwar Sadat, Nasser's successor as Egypt's head of state, a coward after Egypt concluded a cease-fire with Israel to end the 1973 Arab-Israeli war. The same year, Sadat exposed a Libyan plot to torpedo the famous British passenger liner Queen Elizabeth II in the Mediterranean.

In 1977 fierce fighting erupted along the Libya-Egypt border, and it appeared that the two countries were on the brink of a full-scale war. The conflict soon subsided, however, though Sadat continued to assert that Qaddafi had plotted to overthrow the Egyptian government.

Libya, like other Arab countries, severed diplomatic relations with Egypt in 1978, after Sadat agreed to the Camp David Accords, a peace agreement between Egypt and Israel. Qaddafi intensely opposed any Arab accommodation with Israel—a position he has held consistently throughout his time in power. In the fall of 2002, for example, Libya announced its intention to withdraw from the 22-member Arab League. Qaddafi portrayed the action as a protest against "official Arab cowardice" in dealing with Israel and its staunch ally, the United States—which Libya's leader said made him "ashamed to be an Arab."

A DANGEROUS, UNPREDICTABLE ALLY

Qaddafi's militant anti-Israeli and anti-American stance generally found favor among Libya's population, and among some discontented people in other Arab and African nations. In 1979, for example, anti-American protesters attacked and burned the U.S.

embassy in Tripoli (no doubt with the approval of the regime).

At the same time, however, even supporters of Qaddafi tended to keep the Libyan leader at arm's length because of his unpredictability. One small but revealing example was his relationship with the West African country of Upper Volta (now called Burkina Faso) during the early 1980s. In 1982 a military takeover led to the formation of a "People's Salvation Council" to govern Upper Volta, situated 1,000 miles (1,609 km) southwest of Libya in the sub-Saharan interior of the African continent. Qaddafi, who by that time had a small but fervent following among Upper Volta revolutionaries, decided to visit the country. The leader of the People's Salvation Council did not approve of the visit. Shortly afterward, military leaders with pro-Qaddafi leanings were arrested and Libyan technical workers were expelled from Upper Volta. Two years later, an army officer and Qaddafi sympathizer, Captain Thomas Sankara, took control of Upper Volta's government. Neighboring countries expected—and feared—that Sankara would establish formal ties with Libya. Mindful of their concern, however, Sankara adopted a cool stance toward Libya. He pledged not to become a "pawn" of Colonel Qaddafi.

This was during the period when Libyan soldiers occupied much of Chad. While Qaddafi managed to attract support for his Chad territorial claims from scattered radical factions throughout Africa, Chad's neighboring countries were for the most part deeply alarmed by Libya's aggressive tendencies. So were Libya's other neighbors, as well as distant African countries—not to mention Western powers.

In August 1982, Libya was scheduled to host a summit meeting of the Organization of African Unity (OAU)—an association of African nations of which Libya had been a founding member in 1963, when King Idris ruled the country. Qaddafi was to be chairman of the 1982 summit. The governments of Egypt, Sudan, and Somalia, staunchly

Libya and Egypt had a close relationship during the early years of Qaddafi's rule; in fact, Egypt provided some support for the 1969 coup that brought Qaddafi to power, and in 1972 the two countries joined with Syria to form the Federation of Arab Republics, a short-lived pan-Arab union. However, Qaddafi disagreed with Egypt's decision to seek peace with Israel after the 1973 Yom Kippur War, and he broke completely with Egypt after its president, Anwar Sadat (left), signed a peace agreement with Israeli prime minister Menachem Begin (right) that had been negotiated in September 1978 with the help of U.S. president Jimmy Carter.

opposed to Qaddafi's regime, refused to participate. They were joined in their **boycott** by 15 other African nations that disagreed over the proper representation of Chad at the summit. As a result, the OAU summit was not held in Libya. It convened the following year in Ethiopia—and Qaddafi indignantly stayed home.

While occupying portions of Chad, Qaddafi also claimed territory in northern Niger, Chad's western neighbor and Libya's neighbor on its southwestern border. Perhaps not surprisingly, part of this disputed land is known to be rich in uranium. Libya also laid claim to territory in southeastern Algeria.

Meanwhile Qaddafi tried to curry favor with diverse governments, both in Africa and elsewhere. He was particularly drawn to radical revolutionary leaders. During the 1970s he sent soldiers and military supplies to aid Idi Amin, the notoriously brutal dictator of Uganda in equatorial Africa. Thousands of political opponents were executed during Amin's eight-year reign of terror. In 1979 Ugandan guerrillas and forces from neighboring Tanzania defeated Amin's army, forcing him to flee the country. The deposed dictator temporarily took refuge in Tripoli.

In 1980, when Sergeant Samuel K. Doe seized control of Liberia in a military coup, Libya was the first nation to recognize the new government of the tiny West African country. Qaddafi invited members of the new Liberian regime to Tripoli and reportedly offered them large cash incentives to become Libyan allies. But Doe, like Sankara in Upper Volta, understood that to befriend Qaddafi would be to alienate many foreign powers that were supplying his fledgling government with much-needed aid. Doe also understood that to accept assistance from Libya would require him to become part of Qaddafi's grand plan for a unified, Arab-dominated Africa. So he distanced his government from that of Qaddafi.

LIBYA AND THE UNITED STATES

The United States maintained generally cordial relations with Libya under the regime of King Idris. Soon after Muammar Qaddafi took power, however, strains in the relationship emerged, in part because of Qaddafi's militant and uncompromising anti-Israel stance and in part because of his international adventurism.

In 1980 the United States withdrew its foreign embassy from Tripoli (the government of Belgium served as a U.S. intermediary in communications with the Libyan regime); other countries later followed suit. Likewise, Libya did not maintain an embassy (or "people's bureau," as it calls its foreign offices) in the United States.

For the United States, Qaddafi's sponsorship of terrorism was particularly egregious. International terrorist groups operated as many as 20 training bases within Libyan territory, with Qaddafi's blessing.

In 1981 antagonism between Libya and the United States erupted into a military confrontation. Qaddafi claimed the entire Gulf of Sidra as Libyan territorial waters. The United States (and the international community), on the other hand, claimed that Libya's coastal waters extended only to the standard 12-mile (19-km) limit. During U.S. naval exercises inside the Gulf of Sidra—maneuvers many observers considered provocative—Qaddafi ordered air strikes against the American fleet. Two Libyan warplanes were shot down; American forces sustained no damage or casualties. In the wake of the incident, reports circulated that Qaddafi had dispatched a hit squad to kill the U.S. president, Ronald Reagan. Though the reports were later discredited, they probably contributed to the rising tensions between Washington and Tripoli.

In January 1986 Qaddafi issued another challenge to the United States. He proclaimed the northern limit of the Gulf of Sidra a "line of death where we shall stand and fight with our backs to the wall" against any American incursions. In March the United States again responded with naval "exercises," during which carrier-based warplanes crossed Qaddafi's "line of death" and were fired at by Libyan surface-to-air missile batteries. American forces retaliated by sinking two Libyan naval vessels in the area before concluding the Gulf of Sidra maneuvers.

Within a week, however, a bomb exploded in the crowded La Belle discotheque in Berlin, West Germany. The nightclub was a popular spot for U.S. servicemen stationed at a nearby base, and two American soldiers were among the three people killed in the blast; 41 Americans were among the more than 230 wounded. Evidence pointed to Libyan involvement in the terrorist attack.

The Reagan administration responded on April 14 with long-range bombing raids on Libyan bases around Tripoli and Benghazi, including the barracks where Qaddafi himself was living. Libya's leader escaped unscathed, but 40 Libyans were said to have been killed, among them Qaddafi's 18-month-old adopted daughter.

In addition to the air raids, which Reagan administration officials described as "incentives" for Qaddafi to change his behavior, the United States imposed trade sanctions on Libya in 1986.

In the years that followed, however, other terrorist incidents with Libyan connections would occur. The most notable was the December 1988 bombing of Pan American Flight 103 over Lockerbie, Scotland. Killed in the disaster were all 259 passengers and crew members on board the jetliner, along with 11 Scottish citizens on the ground. An international investigation implicated two Libyans in the bombing.

Qaddafi's initial refusal to turn over two suspects—along with his refusal to cooperate in the investigation of a similar incident in which Libyan involvement was suspected, the bombing of a French airliner over Africa—prompted the United Nations to impose limited economic sanctions on Libya in 1992. The UN tightened those sanctions the following year in the face of continued Libyan obstinacy.

In April 1999 Qaddafi's government agreed to cooperate with investigations in the Lockerbie bombing, and turned over the two Libyan suspects. They were tried before a Scottish court convened in the Netherlands. Libya also agreed to pay $2.3 billion to victims' families in 2003, and later paid out other amounts to those associated with other terror attacks. These actions led the UN Security

This sculpture in Tripoli, which shows a Libyan hand crushing a U.S. fighter jet, reflects the contentious relationship between the United States and Libya that existed for several decades.

Council to vote to lift the sanctions in September of that year. In 2006, diplomatic relations between the U.S. and Libya were restored in full.

A NEW DIRECTION?

Some observers have suggested that certain actions by Colonel Qaddafi—including his decision to hand over the Lockerbie suspects and his expressions of sympathy for the American people in the wake of the September 11, 2001, terrorist attacks on the World Trade Center—signaled a shift toward a more moderate and pragmatic Libyan foreign policy. During his early years in power, Libya's oil wealth enabled Qaddafi to adopt a militant, aggressive posture toward neighboring countries and even world superpowers. But decades as an international pariah and the resulting economic toll on his country may have compelled Qaddafi to rethink his policies.

Mansour O. El-Kikhia, in his 1997 book *Libya's Qaddafi: The Politics of Contradiction*, wrote: "As the shadow of poverty, which the country has successfully eluded for the past three decades, reemerges, a more realistic foreign policy will not be a matter of choice; it will be a necessity. . . . Small countries in general and Libya in particular can least afford to 'place all their eggs in one basket,' nor can they afford to antagonize all the military or economic world powers."

Andrew Cockburn, reporting in a November 2000 *National Geographic* article titled "Libya: An End to Isolation," observed changes in the Libyan leader's image as well as an increased openness in Libyan society. Cockburn noted that the aging Qaddafi (who turned 66 in 2008) was perceived by Westerners as less of a "rabble-rouser." And, as he traveled the country in the late 1990s, Cockburn found the Libyan people he met to be "naturally friendly" and willing to speak to foreigners.

In August 2003, in a letter addressed to the United Nations Security Council, Libya accepted full responsibility for the Pan Am 103 bombing. The Libyan government agreed to pay $2.7 billion to the families of its victims. The following year Libya agreed to pay $35 million to the families of victims of the 1986 Berlin disco bombing.

Although the UN lifted its sanctions against Libya in September 2003, the United States maintained its own sanctions against the country, citing Libya's nuclear weapons program as a reason not to resume normal relations. The following December Qaddafi announced that Libya would end its development of biological and chemical weapons, discontinue its nuclear arms program, and

The secretary general of the United Nations Ban Ki-moon (left) meets with Muammar Qaddafi in January 2008. Since renouncing terrorism in 2003, Qaddafi has promoted efforts to reengage Libya with the international community.

allow international weapons inspectors into the country. In response the United States lifted its economic sanctions.

Further normalization of diplomatic relations between Libya and the United States was evident in May 2006, when the U.S. government established a full embassy in Tripoli. The United States also rescinded its designation of Libya as a state sponsor of terrorism. In September 2008 Condoleezza Rice became the first U.S. secretary of state to visit Libya since 1953.

Libya has continued to reengage with the international community. In January 2008 the country began serving on the UN Security Council, representing the Africa group. The following year, Qaddafi was elected chairman of the African Union by leaders meeting in Addis Ababa, Ethiopia.

CHRONOLOGY

ca. 3000 B.C.: Earliest Berbers are thought to have occupied the region of what is now Libya.

ca. 1000 B.C.: Arrival of Phoenician traders in North Africa.

631 B.C.: Greeks establish the port of Cyrene.

146 B.C.: Romans sack Carthage in what is today Tunisia; North Africa feels Roman influence for more than seven centuries.

A.D. 642: Arabs invade Cyrenaica and begin domination of North Africa.

1551: Ottomans capture Tripoli from Spanish Crusaders.

1711: Beginning of the Karamanli era.

1835: Ottoman (Turkish) rule is reestablished.

1911: Italian forces occupy what is now northern Libya. After Turkey gives up its claims in the area the following year, Tripolitania and Cyrenaica become, in effect, Italian colonies.

1914–16: First Italo-Sanusi War.

1923–31: Second Italo-Sanusi War.

1939–45: World War II. During the early years of the war, North Africa is the scene of furious desert fighting between armored forces of the Axis and Allied powers, destroying Libyan cities.

1951: The United Nations recognizes Libya's independence; the rule of King Idris begins.

1959: Oil is discovered in Libya, and the country is quickly transformed from one of Africa's poorest nations to one of its richest.

1969: After he and fellow army officers launch a successful coup, Muammar al-Qaddafi assumes leadership of Libya's government.

1973: Qaddafi proclaims an ongoing "cultural revolution" in Libya.

1979: Libyan protestors attack the U.S. embassy in Tripoli; the following year, the United States closes the embassy and withdraws its diplomats.

1982: The United States stops all exports to Libya except food and medicine.

1986: Accusing Libya of involvement in terrorist activities that killed and injured Americans, the United States bombs targets in Tripoli and Benghazi.

1992–99: United Nations economic sanctions are in effect against Libya.

CHRONOLOGY

2000: Qaddafi announces that Libya's national government has completely turned power over to local authorities.

2002: The U.S. State Department reports that Libya, while still considered a terrorist-supporting state, seems to be distancing itself from world terrorism; Libya announces its decision to withdraw from the Arab League over what it considers the organization's weak position toward Israeli treatment of Palestinians.

2003: In August Libya agrees to pay $2.7 billion to families of those killed in the Pam Am flight 103 bombing; the following month the United Nations Security Council votes to lift sanctions against the country. In December Qaddafi announces that Libya will discontinue its nuclear weapons program.

2004: Libya agrees to pay $35 million to the families of those killed in the 1986 Berlin disco bombing.

2005: Libya holds its first auction of oil and gas exploration licenses to foreign corporations.

2006: In May the United States and Libya restore full diplomatic ties.

2008: Secretary of State Condoleezza Rice visits Libya, becoming the highest-ranking U.S. official to visit the country since 1953.

2009: Libya and the United States exchange ambassadors for the first time since 1973; Qaddafi is elected chairman of the African Union.

GLOSSARY

Bedouin—a nomadic Arab of the desert.

boycott—to refuse to have dealings with an individual, group, or country in protest of a policy or action.

caliph—an Islamic leader considered the successor of the prophet Muhammad.

communism—a political and economic system that, among other characteristics, calls for government ownership of all property and the means of production, and equal distribution of goods.

corsairs—pirates operating along the Barbary Coast of northern Africa in the 18th and 19th centuries.

coup—the sudden or violent overthrow of a government by a small group.

couscous—a food item common in Libya and throughout North Africa, made with wheat flour.

emir—an Islamic ruler, chieftain, or prince.

ghibli—a hot desert wind of northern Africa.

gross domestic product (GDP)—the total value of goods and services produced in a country in a one-year period.

hajj—the pilgrimage to Mecca, which every Muslim is supposed to try to make at least once in his or her lifetime.

imam—a Shiite Muslim leader claiming to be a divinely appointed, infallible successor of Muhammad in the line of Ali; also, the prayer leader of a mosque.

Islamists—fundamentalist Muslims who support the establishment of governments and societies based on a conservative interpretation of the teachings of Islam.

janissaries—Turkish peasants organized into an elite military corp serving the Ottoman Empire.

lahma—a clan, or group of extended families, in Libya.

Maghreb—the western Arab-Islamic world, including the Tripolitania region of Libya.

Mashriq—the eastern Arab-Islamic world; some would mark its westernmost point as the Cyrenaica region of Libya.

minaret—the pointed tower of a mosque.

GLOSSARY

monarchy—rulership of a country by a king (monarch).

mosque—a Muslim house of worship.

muezzin—a mosque official who calls the people to regular prayer.

nomads—wandering people, often herders who move from place to place to find pastures and water for their livestock.

oasis—an isolated fertile area near a reliable source of water in the desert.

pan-Arab—relating to, characteristic of, or advocating the unification of all Arab peoples.

pasha—the governor of a province of North Africa under the Ottomans.

pharaoh—a ruler of ancient Egypt.

qabilah—a tribe, composed of a group of clans.

Sharia—Islamic law.

socialism—a political and economic system that calls for government ownership of business and industry and government supervision of the distribution of goods.

souk—a marketplace in northern Africa or the Middle East; also, a stall in such a marketplace.

totalitarian—relating to, or characteristic of, a government that forcibly controls all aspects of its citizens' lives; dictatorial.

tribute—an ancient form of tax (in the form of money, trade goods, or agricultural produce) paid to acknowledge submission to a dominant ruler or society.

wadi—a dry desert riverbed filled only occasionally and temporarily by rainwater.

FURTHER READING

Ahmida, Ali Abdullatif. *Forgotten Voices: Power and Agency in Colonial and Postcolonial Libya.* New York: Routlege, 2005.

Cockburn, Andrew. "Libya: An End to Isolation." *National Geographic*, November 2000.

Diagram Group. *History of North Africa.* New York: Facts on File, 2003.

Di Piazza, Francesca. *Libya in Pictures.* Minneapolis, Minn.: Lerner, 2005.

Ham, Anthony. *Libya.* New York: Lonely Planet, 2007.

Jones, Roger. *Libya—Culture Smart!: A Quick Guide to Customs and Etiquette.* London: Kuperard, 2008.

Martinez, Luis. *The Libyan Paradox.* New York: Columbia University Press, 2007.

Miller, Debra. *Libya.* San Diego, Calif: Lucent, 2005.

Naden, Corrine and Rose Blue. *Heroes & Villains: Muammar al-Qaddafi.* San Diego, Calif.: Lucent, 2004.

Rogerson, Barnaby. *A Traveller's History of North Africa.* New York: Interlink Publishing Group, 2000.

St John, Ronald Bruce. *Libya: From Colony to Independence.* London: Oneworld, 2008.

Vandewalle, Dirk. *A History of Modern Libya.* Cambridge, U.K.: Cambridge University Press, 2006.

INTERNET RESOURCES

http://allafrica.com/libya

News and other information about Libya.

**https://www.cia.gov/library/publications/the-world-factbook/
geos/ly.html**

The CIA World Factbook Libya page contains statistics and general information.

http://www.libyana.org

Described as a "collective, volunteer effort of a group of Libyan women and men who love their culture and heritage," this website includes brief information on Libya's land, people, and art and features music and images.

http://www.libyaonline.com

Government-sponsored site offers information about Libyan business, arts and literature, travel considerations, and more.

http://www.historycentral.com/nationbynation/

Basic country information regarding geography, government, history, human rights, and so on, with statistics.

http://www.eia.doe.gov/emeu/cabs/Libya/Background.html

U.S. Energy Information Administration website offers details about Libya's oil and natural gas production, exports, and reserves.

http://travel.state.gov/travel/cis_pa_tw/cis/cis_951.html

U.S. Bureau of Government Consular Affairs website provides travel requirements, cautions, and other considerations for those interested in visiting Libya.

INDEX

Abdullah (King), *48*
African Union, *54*, 107
agriculture, 20, 23, 32, 60–63
Akhdar (Green) Mountains, *22*, 23, 24, 26
   See also geographic features
Al Aziziyah, 21
Al-Jifarah Plain, 20, 22, 24
   See also geographic features
Al Khums, 87
al-Qaddafi, Muammar. *See* Qaddafi, Muammar
Ali II, 39
ibn Ali Karamanli, Yusuf, 36–39
Amin, Idi, 102
Arab League, *8*, 46, *97*, 98, 99
arts. *See* culture

el-Badri, Abdallah Salem, *65*
Barbary pirates. *See* corsairs
Bedouin tribes, 40, 45, 75–76, 92
   See also tribal nomads
Begin, Menachem, *101*
Benghazi, 87–88, 104
Benghul, Ali, 36
Berbers, *29*, 30–31, 34, *42*, 51, 71, 74, 82
   See also tribal nomads
Bourguiba, Habib, 97–98
Burkina Faso (Upper Volta), 100
Bush, George W., *106*

calendar, Islamic, 88–89
   See also Islam
Camp David Accords, 99, *101*
capitalism, 14, 16
   See also communism; socialism
Carter, Jimmy, *101*
Carthage, 31, 32, *33*
   See also Phoenicians
Chad, 96, 98–99, 101–102
climate, 20–22, *26*
clothing, 79
   See also culture
communism, 15–16, 56

See also capitalism; socialism
corsairs, 37–38, *39*
culture, 79, *80*, 81–83, 91–93
currency, 59, 60, *61*
   See also economy
Cyrenaica, 22, 23, 24, 31–32, 39, 46–47, 87
   and Italy, 40–43
   oil reserves in, 64
      See also Fezzan; Tripolitania
Cyrene, 31

Darnah, 87
debt, foreign, 64
Doe, Samuel K., 102

economy, 58–65, 105
education, *77*, 78, 81
Egypt, 30–31, 46, 96, 99, *101*
entertainment. *See* culture

Federation of Arab Republics, 96
Fezzan, 22, 23, 24, 41, 45, 71
   See also Cyrenaica; Tripolitania
First Italo-Sanusi War, 40
flag, *56*
food, 91–93
   See also culture
foreign relations, 95–107
France, 38, *98*, 99
Free Unionist Officers, 48
   See also Qaddafi, Muammar

Gadhafi, Mu'ammar. *See* Qaddafi, Muammar
Garamentes, 32, 34
gender roles, 76–79, 92
   and military service, 58, 69
   and religion, 69
General People's Congress (GPC), *16*, 57
   See also government
geographic features, 19–22, 24, 26
geographic regions, tensions among, 46–47
   See also Cyrenaica; Fezzan; Tripolitania

Numbers in **bold italic** refer to captions.

INDEX

Ghanem, Shukri, **65**
ghibli (windstorm), **18**, 19, **26**
government, 14–17, 51, 55–58
Graziani, Rudolfo, 43
    See also Italy
Great Britain, 38, 40, 45, 46, 52
Great Socialist People's Libyan Arab
    Jamahiriya. *See* Libya
Greeks, 31–32
    See also history
Green Book, The, 15, 55, 82–83
Gulf of Sidra, 23, 87, 103–104

health care, 79–81
history
    Berber civilization, 29–31
    and the corsairs, 37–38
    and Islam, 34
    Italian colonization, 40–45
    Libyan independence, 45–49
    Ottoman Empire, 35–37, 38–39
    Phoenician civilization, 31–32
    Roman Empire, 32–34
holidays
    Islamic, 88–90
    national, 91

Idris I (King), **15**, 40–42, 43, 46–48, 52, **59**, 101,
    103
independence, Libyan, 42, 46, **47**, **59**, 75
Islam, **29**, 34, 56, 58, 67–69, 77–79, 91, 93
    and art, 81–82
    holidays of, 88–90
Israeli-Palestinian conflict, **97**, 99–100, **101**
Italo-Sanusi Wars (First and Second), 40, 43
Italo-Turkish War, **41**
Italy, 39–45, 52
    See also history

Karamanli, Ahmad, 35–36
Koran. *See* Qur'an

labor shortages, 66
    See also economy

lahma, 75
    See also tribal nomads
legal system. *See Sharia* (Islamic law)
Leptis Magna, **29**, 31, **86**
Liberia, 102
Libya
    area, 22, **23**, **26**
    borders, 14, 23–24, 26
    cities, 85–88
    climate, 20–22, **26**
    economy, 59–65, 105
    education, **77**, 78, 81
    flag of, **56**
    foreign debt, 64
    foreign relations, 95–107
    geographic features of, 19–22, 24, 26
    government, 14–17, 51, 55–58
    independence, 42, 46, **47**, **59**, 75
    maps, **25**, **36**, **73**
    military, **54**, 55, 58–59, 69
    population, 22, 71, **72**, **73**, 75
    and the United States, 37–38, **39**, 58–59, **82**,
        91, **94–95**, **98**, 99, 100, 103–107
    wildlife, 26–27
    See also Cyrenaica; Fezzan; Tripolitania
Libyan Arab Force, **47**
literacy rate, **72**, 81
    See also education
Lockerbie (Scotland), **53**, 54, 104–105
    See also terrorism

Maghreb, 24, 35
    See also Tripolitania
maps
    of Libya, **25**, **36**, **73**
Marsa al-Burayqah, 65, 87
Mashriq, 24
    See also Cyrenaica
Mecca, 67, 89–90
    See also Islam
al-Megrahi, Abdelbaset Ali, 105
military, **54**, 55, 58–59, 69, 77
Misratah, 81, 87, **92**
Muhammad, 67, 89

See also Islam

Muhammad Idris al Mahdi as-Sanusi. See Idris I
(King)

al-Mukhtar, Umar, 43

Mussolini, Benito, 43–44

See also Italy

Nafusah Plateau, 24

See also geographic features

Nasser, Gamal Abdel, 49, 96, 99

nationalism. See independence, Libyan

natural resources, 61, 63–64, 65–66

See also oil

an Numayri, Jaafar, 98

oil, *12*, 13, *25*, 46–47, 49, 53, 66, 80, 87, 105

and Idris I, 52

and the Libyan economy, 59, 60, 63–65

Organization of African Unity (OAU), 101–102

Organization of Petroleum Exporting
Countries (OPEC), 64, **65**

See also oil

Ottoman Empire, 35–37, 38–39

See also history

Palestine Liberation Organization (PLO), 53

Pan Am Flight 103, **53**, 54, 104–105, 106

See also terrorism

Pasha, Sinan, 35

petroleum. See oil

Phoenicians, *29*, 31–32, 37, **86**

See also history

pirates, Barbary. See corsairs

population, 22, 71, **72**, **73**, 85

distribution of the, 75

Punic civilization. See Phoenicians

qabilah, 75

See also tribal nomads

Qaddafi, Muammar, 13–17, **48**, 49, 51–60, 63,
66, 68–69, 72, 80, 82–83, 91, 93

and foreign affairs, 96–97, 98–107

and terrorism, 95, 96–97, 103, 104–105, 107

Qadhafi, Moammar. See Qaddafi, Muammar

Qaramanli, Ahmad. See Karamanli, Ahmad

Qasr al-Ghashir, **74**

Qur'an, 67–69, 82, 90

See also Islam

rainfall, 22

See also climate

Reagan, Ronald, 103, 104

religion. See Islam

Rice, Condoleezza, 107

Roman Empire, 14, **29**, 31–33, 85–86

See also history

Sadat, Anwar, 99, **101**

Safar, Suleiman, 35

Sahara Desert, 19–20, **21**, 76

Sankara, Thomas, 100, 102

al-Sanusi, King Idris. See Idris I (King)

Second Italo-Sanusi War, 43

Sharia (Islamic law), 56, 58, **68**

See also Islam

ash Sharif, Ahmad, 40

Shiite Muslims, 67–68

See also Islam

slavery, 71–72

socialism, 14–15, 55–56, 59–60

See also government; *Green Book, The*

Soviet Union, 46, 59

Sudan, 98

Suez Canal, **44**, 46

Sunni Muslims, 67–68

See also Islam

Tadrart Acacus, **30**

terrorism, *16*, 17, 49, 53–54, 60, 95, 96–97,
103–105, **106**, 107

Third International Theory, 56

Tobruk, 87

tourism, 72

transportation system, 88

tribal nomads, 72, 74–75

See also Bedouin tribes; Berbers; Tuareg
nomads

Tripoli, 23, 31, 35, 38–39, **84**, 85–86, 87–88, **89**,

INDEX

100
  and Italy, 39–40
  U.S. bombing of, **94–95**, 104
Tripolitania, 22, 23, 24, 32, 39, 71, 75
  and Italy, 41, 42–43
  oil reserves in, 64
  See also Cyrenaica; Fezzan
Tuareg nomads, 71, 76, **77**
  See also tribal nomads
Tunisia, 96–98
Turkey, 39–40, 52

United Nations, **13**, 45–46, 49, **97**, 107
  economic sanctions of, 60, 104–106
  security council, 106, 107

United States, 37–38, **39**, 46, 58–59, **82**, 91,
  94–95, **98**, 99, 100, 103–107
Upper Volta (Burkina Faso), 100, 102
USSR. *See* Soviet Union

Vandals, 33–34

water resources, 13, 20, 63
wildlife, 26–27
World War I, 36, 40, 46
World War II, **44**, 45, **47**, 52

Yusuf (Yusuf ibn Ali Karamanli), 36–39

Zuwarah, 87

PICTURE CREDITS

CONTRIBUTORS

The **FOREIGN POLICY RESEARCH INSTITUTE (FPRI)** served as editorial consultants for the MAJOR MUSLIM NATIONS series. FPRI is one of the nation's oldest "think tanks." The Institute's Middle East Program focuses on Gulf security, monitors the Arab-Israeli peace process, and sponsors an annual conference for teachers on the Middle East, plus periodic briefings on key developments in the region.

Among the FPRI's trustees is a former Secretary of State and a former Secretary of the Navy (and among the FPRI's former trustees and interns, two current Undersecretaries of Defense), not to mention two university presidents emeritus, a foundation president, and several active or retired corporate CEOs.

The scholars of FPRI include a former aide to three U.S. Secretaries of State, a Pulitzer Prize–winning historian, a former president of Swarthmore College and a Bancroft Prize–winning historian, and two former staff members of the National Security Council. And the FPRI counts among its extended network of scholars— especially its Inter-University Study Groups—representatives of diverse disciplines, including political science, history, economics, law, management, religion, sociology, and psychology.

DR. HARVEY SICHERMAN is president and director of the Foreign Policy Research Institute in Philadelphia, Pennsylvania. He has extensive experience in writing, research, and analysis of U.S. foreign and national security policy, both in government and out. He served as Special Assistant to Secretary of State Alexander M. Haig Jr. and as a member of the Policy Planning Staff of Secretary of State James A. Baker III. Dr. Sicherman was also a consultant to Secretary of the Navy John F. Lehman Jr. (1982–1987) and Secretary of State George Shultz (1988).

A graduate of the University of Scranton (B.S., History, 1966), Dr. Sicherman earned his Ph.D. at the University of Pennsylvania (Political Science, 1971), where he received a Salvatori Fellowship. He is author or editor of numerous books and articles, including *America the Vulnerable: Our Military Problems and How to Fix Them* (FPRI, 2002) and *Palestinian Autonomy, Self-Government and Peace* (Westview Press, 1993). He edits *Peacefacts*, an FPRI bulletin that monitors the Arab-Israeli peace process.

DANIEL E. HARMON is an author and editor in Spartanburg, South Carolina. He has written more than 30 nonfiction books, one short story collection, and numerous magazine and newspaper articles. Harmon has served for many years as associate editor of *Sandlapper: The Magazine of South Carolina* and editor of *The Lawyer's PC,* a national computer newsletter published by West Group. His special interests include nautical history and folk music.